Alice Brown

The day of his youth

Alice Brown

The day of his youth

ISBN/EAN: 9783742894298

Manufactured in Europe, USA, Canada, Australia, Japa

Cover: Foto ©Lupo / pixelio.de

Manufactured and distributed by brebook publishing software (www.brebook.com)

Alice Brown

The day of his youth

THE DAY OF HIS YOUTH

BY
ALICE BROWN

BOSTON AND NEW YORK
HOUGHTON MIFFLIN COMPANY
The Riverside Press Cambridge

THE DAY OF HIS YOUTH

THE life of Francis Hume began in an old yet very real tragedy. His mother, a lovely young woman, died at the birth of her child: an event of everyday significance, if you judge by tables of mortality and the probabilities of being. She was the wife of a man well-known among honored American names, and her death made more than the usual ripple of nearer pain and wider condolence. To the young husband it was an afflicting calamity, entirely surprising even to those who were themselves acquainted with grief. He was not merely rebellious and wildly distraught, in the way of mourners. He sank into a cold sedateness of change. His life forsook its accustomed channels. Vividly alive to the one bright point still burning in the past, toward the present world he seemed absolutely benumbed. Yet certain latent conceptions of the real values of existence must have sprung up in him, and protested against days to be thereafter dominated by artificial restraints. He had lost his hold on life. He had even acquired a sudden distaste for it; but his previous knowledge of beauty and perfection would not suffer him to shut himself up in a cell of reserve, and isolate himself thus from his kind. He could become a hermit, but only under the larger conditions of being. He had the firmest conviction that he could never grow any more; yet an imperative voice within bade him seek the highest outlook in which growth is possible. He had formed a habit of beautiful living, though in no sense a living for any other save the dual soul now withdrawn; and he could not be satisfied with lesser loves, the makeshifts of a barren life. So, turning from the world, he fled into

THE DAY OF HIS YOUTH

the woods; for at that time Nature seemed to him the only great, and he resolved that Francis, the son, should be nourished by her alone.

One spring day, when the boy was eight years old, his father had said to him:—

"We are going into the country to sleep in a tent, catch our own fish, cook it ourselves, and ask favors of no man."

"Camping!" cried the boy, in ecstasy.

"No; living."

The necessities of a simple life were got together, and supplemented by other greater necessities, — books, pictures, the boy's violin, — and they betook themselves to a spot where the summer visitor was yet unknown, the shore of a lake stretching a silver finger toward the north. There they lived all summer, shut off from human intercourse save with old Pierre, who brought their milk and eggs and constituted their messenger-in-ordinary to the village, ten miles away.

THE DAY OF HIS YOUTH

When autumn came, Ernest Hume looked into his son's brown eyes and asked, —

"Now shall we go back?"

"No! no! no!" cried the boy, with a child's passionate cumulation of accent.

"Not when the snow comes?"

"No, father."

"And the lake is frozen over?"

"No, father."

"Then," said Hume, with a sigh of great content, "we must have a log-cabin, lest our bones lie bleaching on the shore."

Next morning he went into the woods with Pierre and two men hastily summoned from the village, and there they began to make axe-music, the requiem of the trees. The boy sat by, dreaming as he sometimes did for hours before starting up to throw himself into the active delights of swimming, leaping, or rowing a boat. Next day, also, they kept on cutting into the heart of the forest. One dryad after another was despoiled of her shelter; one after another, the green tents of the bird and the wind were folded to make that sacred tabernacle — a home. Sometimes Francis chopped a little with his hatchet, not to be left out of the play, and then sat by again, smoothing the bruised fern-forests, or whistling back the squirrels who freely chattered out their opinions on invasion. Then came other days just as mild winds were fanning the forest into gold, when the logs went groaning through the woods, after slow-stepping horses, to be piled into symmetry, tightened with plaster, and capped by a roof. This, windowed, swept and garnished, with a central fireplace wherein two fires could flame and roar, was the log-cabin. This was home. The hired builders had protested against its primitive form; they sighed for a snug frame house, French roof and bay windows. "'Ware the cold!" was their daily croak.

"We'll live in fur and toughen ourselves," said Ernest Hume. And turning to his boy that night, when they sat together by their own fire, he asked, —

"Shall we fashion our muscles into steel, our skin into armor? Shall we make our eyes strong enough to face the sun by day, and pure enough to meet the chilly stars at night? Shall we have Nature for our only love? Tell me, sir!"

And Francis, who hung upon his father's voice, even when the words were beyond him, answered, "Yes, father, please!" and went on feeding birch strips to the fire, where they turned from vellum to mysterious missals blazoned by an unseen hand.

The idyl continued unbroken for twelve years. Yet it was not wholly idyllic, for, even with money multiplying for them out in the world, there were hard personal conditions against which they had to fight. Ernest Hume delighted in the fierceness of the winter wind, the cold resistance of the snow; cut off, as he

THE DAY OF HIS YOUTH

honestly felt himself to be, from spiritual growth, he had great joy in strengthening his physical being until it waxed into insolent might. Francis, too, took so happily to the stern yet lovely phases of their life that his father never thought of possible wrong to him in so shaping his early years. As for Ernest Hume, he had bound himself the more irrevocably to right living by renouncing artificial bonds. He had removed his son from the world, and he had thereby taken upon himself the necessity of becoming a better world. Therefore he did not allow himself in any sense to rust out. He did a colossal amount of mental burnishing; and, a gentleman by nature, he adopted a daily purity of speech and courtesy of manner which were less like civilized life than the efflorescence of chivalry at its best. He had chosen for himself a part; by his will, a Round Table sprang up in the woods, though two knights only were to hold counsel there.

THE DAY OF HIS YOUTH

The conclusion of the story — so far as a story is ever concluded — must be found in the words of Francis Hume. Before he was twenty, his strength began stirring within him, and he awoke, not to any definite discontent, but to that fever of unrest which has no name. Possibly a lad of different temperament might not have kept housed so long; but he was apparently dreamy, reflective, in love with simple pleasures, and, though a splendid young animal, inspired and subdued by a thrilling quality of soul. And he woke up. How he awoke may be learned only from his letters.

These papers have, by one of the incredible chances of life, come into my hands. I see no possible wrong in their publication, for now the Humes are dead, father and son; nay, even the name adopted here was not their own. They were two slight bubbles of being, destined to rise, to float for a time, and to be again resolved into the unknown sea. Yet while they lived, they were iridescent; the colors of a far-away sun played upon them, and they sent him back his gleams. To lose them wholly out of life were some pain to those of us who have been privileged to love them through their own written confessions. So here are they given back to the world which in no other way could adequately know them.

I NEVER had a friend! Did any human creature twenty years old ever write that before, unless he did it in a spirit of bitterness because he was out of humor with his world? Yet I can say it, knowing it to be the truth. My father and I are one, the oak and its branch, the fern and its fruitage; but for somebody to be the mirror of my own thoughts,

---

* This title is adopted by the editor that the narrative may be at least approximately clear. The paragraphs headed thus were scribblings on loose sheets: a sort of desultory journal.

tantalizingly strange, intoxicatingly new, where shall I look? Ah, but I know! I will create him from my own longings. He shall be born of the blood and sinew of my brain and heart. Stand forth, beautiful one, made in the image of my fancy, and I will tell thee all — all I am ashamed to tell my father, and tired of imprisoning in my own soul. What shall I call thee? Friend: that will be enough, all-comprehending and rich in joy. To-day I have needed thee more than ever, though it is only to-day that I learned to recognize the need. All the morning a sweet languor held me, warm, like the sun, and touched with his fervor, so that I felt within me darts of impelling fire. I sat in the woods by the spring, my eyes on the dancing shadows at my feet, not thinking, not willing, yet expectant. I felt as if something were coming, and that I must be ready to meet it when the great moment should strike. Suddenly my heart beat high in snatches of rhythm;

my feet stirred, my ears woke to the whir of wings, and my eyes to flickering shade. My whole self was whelmed and suffocated in a wave of sweet delight. And then it was that my heart cried out for another heart to beat beside it and make harmony for the two; then it was that thou, dear one, wast born from my thought. I am not disloyal in seeking companionship. My father is myself. Let me say that over and over. When I tell him my fancies, he smiles sadly, saying they are the buds of youth, born never to flower. To him Nature is goddess and mother; he turns to her for sustenance by day, and lies on her bosom at night. After death he will be content to rest in her arms and become one flesh with her mould. But I — I! O, is it because I am young; and will the days chill out this strange, sweet fever, as they have in him? Two years ago — yes, a year — I had no higher joy than to throw myself, body and soul, into motion: to row, fish, swim,

THE DAY OF HIS YOUTH

to listen, in a dream of happiness, while my father read old Homer to me in the evening, or we masterfully swept through duets — 'cello and violin — that my sleep was too dreamless to repeat to me. And now the very world is changed; help me to understand it, my friend; or, if I am to blame, help me to conquer myself.

II

I have much to tell thee, my friend! and of a nature never before known in these woods and by this water. Last night, at sunset, I stood on the Point waiting for my father to come in from his round about the island, when suddenly a boat shot out from Silver Stream and came on toward me, rowed to the accompaniment of a song I never heard. I stood waiting, for the voices were beautiful, one high and strong (and as I listened, it flashed upon me that my father had said the 'cello is like a woman singing), another, deep and rich. There were two men, as I saw when they neared me, and two women; and all were young. The men — what were they like? I hardly know, except that they made me feel ashamed of my roughness. And the women! One was yellow-haired and pale; she had a fairy build, I think, and her shoulders were like the birch-tree. Her head was bare, and the sun — he had stayed to do it — had turned all the threads to gold. She was so white! white as the tiarella in the spring. When I saw her, I bent forward; they looked my way, and I drew back behind the tree. I had been curious, and I was ashamed; it seemed to me they might stop and say, "Who is this fellow who lives in the woods and stares at people like an owl by night?" But the oars dipped, and the boat and song went on. The song! if I but knew it! It called my feet to dancing. It was like laughter and the play of the young squirrels. I watched for them to go back, and in an hour they did, still singing in jubilant chorus; and after that came my father. As soon as I saw him, I knew something had happened. I have never seen him so sad, so weary. He put his hand on my shoulder, after we had beached the boat and were walking up to the cabin.

"Francis," he said, "our good days are over."

"Why?" I asked.

It appeared to me, for some reason, that they had just begun; perhaps because the night was so fragrant and the stars so near. The world had never seemed so homelike and so warm. I knew how a bird feels in its own soft nest.

"Because some people have come to camp on the Bay Shore. I saw their tents, and asked Pierre. He says they are here for the summer. Fool! fool that I was, not to buy that land!"

"But perhaps we shall like them!" I

said, and my voice choked in the saying, the world seemed so good, so strange. He grasped my shoulder, and his fingers felt like steel. "Boy! boy!" he whispered. For a minute, I fancied he was crying, as I cried once, years ago, when my rabbit died. "I knew it would come," he said. "Kismet! I bow the neck. Put thy foot upon it gently, if may be."

We went on to the cabin, but somehow we could not talk; and it was not long before my father sought his tent. I went also to mine, and lay down as I was: but not to sleep. Those voices sang in my ears, and my heart beat till it choked me. Outside, the moon was at full flood, and I could bear it no longer. I crept softly out of my tent, and ran — lightly, so that my father should not hear, but still swiftly — to the beach. I pushed off a boat, grudging every grating pebble, and dipped my oars carefully, not to be heard. My father would not have cared, for often I go out at midnight; but I felt strangely.

Yet I knew I must see those tents. Out of his earshot, I rowed in hot haste, and every looming tree on the wooded bank seemed to whisper "Hurry! hurry!" I rounded the Point in a new agony lest I should never hear those singing voices again; and there lay the tents, white in the moonlight. I rowed into the shadow of a cliff, tied my boat, and crept along the shore. I could see my mates, and they were mad with fun. Perhaps a dozen people stood there together on the sand laughing, inciting one another to some merrier deed. I stayed in the shadow of my tree, watching them. Then five who were in bathing-dress began wading, and struck out swimming lazily. She was there, the slight, young creature, now with her hair in a glory below her waist. The jealous dark had hid its gold, but I knew what it would be by day. They swam about, calling and laughing in delicious tones, while those on the bank — older people I think — challenged and cautioned them. Then a cry went up, "The raft! the raft!" and they began swimming out, while the women on the bank urged them not to dive, but to wait until to-morrow. I thought I had seen all the sports of young creatures, but I never dreamed of anything so full of happy delight in life as that one girl who climbed on the raft without touching the hand a man offered to help her, and danced about on it, laughing like a woodthrush gone mad with joy, while the other women shrieked in foolish snatches. Then a man dived from the raft, and another. A woman called from shore, "Don't dive, Zoe, to-night!" and suddenly I knew she was Zoe, and that she would dive and that I must be with her. I knocked off my shoes, waded out, still in the shadow, and swam toward the raft. As I neared it, there was one splash after another; then they were coming up, and I was among them. It seemed as if I had dreamed it, and knew how it would all happen; for when her head, sleek as polished metal, came up beside me, I knew it would, and that I should grasp her dress and swim back with her to land. She was surprised; but quite mechanically she swam beside me.

"Let me alone, Tom," she said at last. "I don't want to go in." I had guided her down the bank to my shadowy covert, and there we rose on our feet in shallow water. Then she turned and looked at me. I was not Tom. I was a stranger. I wondered if she would be frightened, if it was a woman's way to scream; and, still worse, if the others would come. I felt that if they did come to mar that one moment, I should kill them. But she was scarcely even surprised. I saw a quiver at the corner of her mouth.

"Will you tell me who you are?" she asked, in a very soft, cool voice.

"You must never dive again from that raft," said I, and my own voice sounded rough and hard. "Pierre knew better

THE DAY OF HIS YOUTH

than to let you anchor it there. The water is too shallow. There are rocks."

"You are the hermit's son!" quite as if she had not heard me, and still looking at me with a little smile.

"You have been in the water long enough," said I. "Go to your tent at once and dress. In another minute you will be shivering."

At that she broke into laughter; it was like the moonlight ripple of the lake.

"Sir, I obey," she said with a mock humility which enchanted me. "Goodnight." She walked up the bank, her wet skirt dripping as she went. I stood dazed, foolish, looking after. Then as she threaded among the trees toward the glimmer of a tent, I recovered myself and ran after her.

"Tell me," I said in haste, "tell me, are you Zoe?"

She was walking on, and I kept pace with her, knowing how rash I was to follow. She turned her head.

"Not to you," she answered, without pausing in her walk. "Good-night!" and she was gone.

I know I found my boat, and that, as I rowed away, there were cries of "Zoe!" from the swimmers who had missed her. I was dripping, but my blood ran fast. Was she cold? Was she shivering? Fools, to let so delicate a creature go into the water at night! The men were fools.

III

Ask me now what of the night and what of the day, for I am the watchman who is fixing his eyes upon life and finding it good. Again I knew there were events in the wind. This morning my father, too, was uneasy, and when we had finished our work, we went out together to the grove near the landing, each with a book; but we did not read. He watched the lake, and I tried not to listen for the dip of oars. At last it came, — O happy sound! — and when I started up, I found his glance upon me.

"Yes, they are coming," he said sadly, bitterly. "It seems we both expected it."

I could not answer, for I do not understand him. Why should it be a grief to him more than to me, this seeing men and women who talk and laugh, with whom one could say all one thought without being misunderstood, and who can bring us such news of the world? But I had not time to say these things, for they were coming, two boatloads of them; and I ran down to the landing to meet them. She was in the first boat, her hair covered now, but kissed by the sun wherever he could reach it. With her was an older woman, the brown-eyed young one, and the same young men. The boat touched the landing, and I helped the other women ashore; but she put her fingers on the shoulder of a man in the boat and stepped past me. Why? why? my heart cried out to her. Does she hate me for last night? Am I so different from her people because I live in the woods? In the moment I hesitated, thinking it over, they all got on shore, and were standing about my father and talking to him. Then I found he had known them, years ago.

"You have changed," the older woman was saying. "You are sadder, but not so bitter."

"That must be because of my son," he said. And he turned to me, and named me to them, and I heard their names. She is Zoe Montrose, the older woman is her aunt, and the two men her cousins; the others, all young, all laughing, and looking and moving about like birds, are friends.

"Do you mean to say you have brought him up in this wilderness?" asked Mrs. Montrose in a whisper I heard. "He is perfect." And then she added, after a quick glance at my face, "Quite perfect, for he can blush."

THE DAY OF HIS YOUTH

My father turned aside as if he had no stomach for soft speeches, and asked them to sit on the bank, because it was pleasanter out of doors. And though Mrs. Montrose said plainly that she wished to see how we lived, he only smiled and led her to a seat under a tree. No one can withstand my father. It seems to me, now that I see him with other people, that he is far finer, more courteous, more commanding than any of them.

"Bring us the wine, Francis," he said to me, and I went in to find he had set it out on a salver in a beautiful decanter I had never seen, and that there were glasses and bits of bread all ready, as if he had expected guests. I brought it out, and then went back for the little glasses; and my father served them all. She held her glass in her hand, and I feared she would not drink; but suddenly, behind the others, she lifted the glass, bowed to me, and a quick smile ran over her face. And then she set it to her lips, still looking at me. It was I who took the glasses away, and hers, which had not been emptied, I left inside my tent. (O, you know, my friend, my other self, what these things are to me! only you! only you!)

"This is Homeric," said Mrs. Montrose. "Bread and wine. The flesh is happily absent."

"Did you expect the blood of 'muttons, beefs, or goats'?" asked my father. "Sacrifice may come later."

Then followed a great deal of talk; but I have not been used to hearing so many people speaking at once, and I could scarcely follow, and cannot at all remember it. But while I sat fearing every instant that they would go, my heart bounded again, for Mrs. Montrose asked us both to row over to their camp and lunch with them. My father at once refused, sternly I thought, but he added, without looking at me, —

"I cannot answer for my son."

THE DAY OF HIS YOUTH

"O, yes, I will go," I cried. I must have been very eager, for they all laughed; all except my father, and he replied, "So be it."

They said good-by to him, and fluttered down to the wharf; and I pushed off my boat with the rest.

"Good-by!" I called to him, but he only waved his hand and turned away.

CERTAINLY I meant every word I said. The moment I saw what you had written for that stupid game, I knew you had a marvelous facility of expression. No doubt your father has nourished it by making you write so many reams of criticism; but it is evident that you had a gift in the beginning, the golden gift in the hand. And so, as I am one who thinks no fortune happier than that of the artisan trained to hammer out a phrase, what is more natural than that I should long for you

From Zoe Montrose to Francis Hume

to ascend from prentice to workman? Therefore write me, — "every day i' the hour," if you will, — and by all means drop the letters in the hollow tree. Here in this forest is the happy reverse of the world-shield; let conventions also be turned topsy-turvy, and letter-carriers be eschewed for a box of living oak and a cushion of crumbling mould. I will be your playmate, your comrade; not your friend. I hate the word between men and women. It is a mantle for mawkish sentiment, the kind that stalks about solemnly like a Puritan at a play, seeing all and affecting his own superiority. But, an you will, be my comrade only; let the Forest of Arden spring up again greenly, and let us play at simplicity and outspoken joy; all for the sake of developing your style! But, first of all, I do not like your reason for asking me to write to you; you cannot see me alone, forsooth! and you have a thousand questions which the others give us no time to ask and answer. Nonsense, doubled and trebled! You know enough of me. Be content to take me as I seem, and not as I am in the world's eyes and in my own; then you will the longer think me worthy to walk your Arden Forest. Not that I have anything to conceal. I am no more very bad than very good; but it is the tragic consequence of living in this world that (especially if we be men! you, sir, I mean you!) we idealize and then weigh — admire, laud to the skies, and then shove under the lens — only to find that all flesh is dust, and differeth not, except so much as sea-sand and mountain-loam. So be content to know this only about me: that I am five years your senior (a quarter-century, ye gods!), that I am poor and once was ambitious; that I earned my bread, as governess and intermittent literary hack, until a year ago, when a tiny fortune was left me by a relative whom the immortals loved not, since he lived so long; that I have written three novels, moderately successful, and am burning to find out whether I can write a play; and, last of all, that my aunt invited me down here to spend this summer in what she calls communion with nature. There! the chapter is closed. Be egotistical, you; but suffer me to talk about things seen and heard, not of those pertaining to the particle Me. Tell me everything you will, and without restraint. I may not criticise your style, though I shall watch to see it develop into something fine.

Francis Hume to Zoe Montrose

YOUR letter! no, mine, as nothing has ever been mine since I was born, for it was conceived for me and moulded for my eyes only. The words you have said to me, even in those long hours on the lake, under the rose of sunset, are tantalizingly lost, though I try to recall them as I lie at night looking at the sky from my bed; I know their sense, their sound, yet something sweetly personal is gone, like a fragrance escaped. This is mine: transcript of your beautiful soul upon a page less white. But though we talk all day on the lake and half the night by camp-fires under the moon, what can I say to you on this cold paper and with this dull pen? Ah, but the thoughts I send you! The winged invisible messengers that go speeding between us in those silent hours when my father sleeps, and I lie in my tent watching the solemn top of the great pine, and over it the stars! Those messages will never be told; earth has no speech for them. They are beyond the scope of music. Yet there must be speech for them somewhere. They are like the overtones we cannot hear unless our ears are delicately attuned; and if you, in your tent, were lying in an ecstasy of waiting for them as I in a rapture of sending, then would you not hear? But the thought is too great, too terrible.

That would be as if we were gods, to taste no more of earthly chills and languors. Do you know what has happened to me since I saw you first? I have grown blind to the rest of this little world. My father's voice sounds far-off and hollow; even his face is strange, as if half hidden by a mist. I do not see the others at your camp, even though they and all their ways ought to be deliciously new to me, like another language. Only when some one touches your hand, or gives you a flower, or treats you familiarly! Then a sudden passion of hatred for the whole world shakes me to the centre, and I long to seize you in my arms, and speed away with you, along the lake and over the hills. I am, in my own eyes, what I have always supposed savages to be; perhaps I am a savage. But there is one agony you might spare me: the story of your life before you came here. Twenty wasted years, and I did not know you! Spring after spring and snow upon snow, when, like an earthborn beast, I was living here in content, rowing, skating, talking with the birds, and you, not fifty miles away, had risen like a star and were gleaming there in that inaccessible heaven. That this should be so, that I must accept it, is terrible to me; but to hear the story of it is like a foretaste of death. It fascinates, it draws me, and yet it kills. That you should say "we" over and over again, when you talk of the music you have heard, the books you have read, is more than I can bear. But I would not have you cease. I must know all, all; and yet it tortures.

FRANKLY, I don't at all like the tone of your letter. I like it as little as I approve your fashion of treating me "before folks." You glower upon me; half as if I were daughter of the sun and you his priest, and half Circassian slave. I don't like it! I came here

Zoe Montrose to Francis Hume

to these solitudes for rest and mental peace. My mind is lying fallow. Should it waken to any immediate fertility, I don't want to expend it on you, either in antiphonal sentiment or in staving off heroics. To speak brutally, I want it for the publisher and mine own after-glory. If this plain statement of the case does n't blight the peach-blossoms of your fancy, I don't know what will. Write me about your life here, the life of the woods and lake. You know enough bird-lore never learned from books to write a thousand St. Francis sermons. Even the fish have told you secrets. I fancy they think you some strange, fresh-water whale not to be accounted for. Tell me about them; and drop this mawkish sentiment caught from books.

Francis Hume to Zoe Montrose

I HAVE read your last letter, but I only half understand you, and I must wholly disobey. For I have learned the meaning of all things created, the sky and the earth, the stars that are the habitations of loving angels, and the worm who seeks his mate. I love you! It is that for which I have lived my twenty years. At last, without warning, my life has flowered, and the fragrance of the blossom intoxicates me, its color blinds. At first I only knew the earth was changed, and that I could never be the same; but I did not translate the knowledge. All the poets had not told me enough; Shakespeare had not prepared me. But last night — do I ever sleep now? — when I lay thinking, thinking, and always of you, my soul spoke and said to me, "So great a thing must be eternal. This longing is like a Beethoven Sonata; it will live and live, growing in glory and color, through the ages, even if it live in your soul alone." And I woke to the sense of it all, and spoke aloud: "It is love!" It is like having a treasure given me to be all my own; for now I have a word for happy use, and I can say over and over, "I love you," and so tell you all. I can whisper "Beloved" in the brief pauses when the others are with us and I have only the chance of a word in your ear. But let me see you next alone. Let me look into your eyes, and demand whether your soul also has had revelation of the truth.

Zoe Montrose to Francis Hume

I ASK myself whether this had to come to you so soon, and whether I could have prevented it. I am afraid not. You were bound to fancy the first woman you met, and that woman chanced to be Zoe Montrose. I know exactly how it was. I have yellow hair, and the sun shone on it. There is always a reason, if one could follow it far enough. It might have been Clara. She was with me in the boat, if you remember; only the sun struck her hair at a different angle, and you never discovered how red it is in

THE DAY OF HIS YOUTH

the hollows, how like leaf mould without. *Bismillah!* the gods have selected me for your enlightenment, and their will be done. I am glad for you in one particular only. I am a worldly woman, filled from the crown to the toe topful of earthly wisdom; but I am not of those sentimental sirens who, in the strictest good-breeding, turn men into beasts by dallying with their worship, and then leaving them high and dry on the rock of disillusionment. I am honest, and I will sweep away your cobwebs in the beginning. My dear, there is no such thing as love as you conceive it. What you and the other poets have seen is a will-o'-the-wisp, created, heaven knows why, save that we may learn hard lessons and that the world may be peopled. You feel for me an ecstasy of devotion. You think it will be eternal; that you were made for me and I for you, and that our two souls will sail forever on in each other's company, chanting pretty trifles

THE DAY OF HIS YOUTH

by the way. God bless and save you! this is the very hyperbole of the poets, and of poets under forty at that. What dominates you is a fever of the blood, an attendant delirium of the mind solely depending on your youth and my passable prettiness. I wish you might have been saved; but it had to happen. I wish, too, that the attack might leave you lightly; but that, also, owing to your unfortunate temperament, is impossible. I can only show my real liking for you by acting sedately, and sitting by your bedside until you rise up sane again and put your hand to the world's work. Do you want this emotion you call love translated to you by a woman who has studied her kind as you study the birds? You say it is, it must be (O, most pitiful cry of the finite after infinity!) eternal. It is nothing of the sort. It is prosaically and sordidly of this earth, especially in the case of men. I grant you that many women do subordinate their lives to what

THE DAY OF HIS YOUTH

they call a great passion (poor Amelia crying over George's picture! O sad, true travesty of the worship we so exalt!), but it is because they have fewer interests, and because tradition has glorified feminine faithfulness and society built its temples on woman's chastity. But men! I know them. Do not expect me to own, for a moment, that any man is going to worship any woman all his life long with the fervor he shows in pursuing the game. Many are kind, some are tender, even to gray hairs and the grave; but that particular form of idolatry which you offer me like a jewel in a case, — it turns to paste in less than ten years, and I will have none of it. But why, you ask, set myself outside the pale of human kind? It is a joy, though fleeting, and if others prize it, even briefly, why not I? I know myself too well. I am, in many ways, a hard woman. My heart is bedded in a crust of flint, and no daw shall peck at it. But if that armor were worn away, if I did sink my traditions to become all-womanly, if I pinned life and soul and faith and breath to a man — O, I shudder to think of seeing that morning-glow fade into the light of common day. It is such women as I who break their hearts; not your sentimental miss who goes puling about, prating love and religion, and confiding in her pastor. I have laughed long at what I call sentiment, but I am more sentimental than the sentimentalist. I own the awful power of one soul over its opposite; but it is a power to which I will not give way. Now, in plain words, what should be the outcome of love? Marriage. And marriage; what of that? It is a welding of two souls, say you, before an altar where a sacred fire is ever after to be kept burning. According to my idea, gathered from observation, it is a business partnership gilded by certain pretty fictions which no one pretends to observe. For six months, a year, five years, the husband worships his wife with

THE DAY OF HIS YOUTH

an ideality which ought to turn beggar-maids to queens and queens to angels. Then, plainly, he gets used to her. She is a very good woman, but her like has been seen before, and may be again. His nature has a dozen sides to be satisfied; he is ambitious, he loves art, or money, or his dirty fellow-men. All very well, you say; without such bent, souls would be cramped and torpid. Ah, but meantime the altar-fire dies down! If she loves him truly, —

> "And if, ah woe! she loves alone,"

she tends it with her poor, weak hands; but no longer are the ministrants two. The little observances of love are forgotten, or they degenerate into a meaningless form more pitiful than silence. You grant, I suppose, that there is a higher life to be sought, one of aspiration, or holy companionship in great deeds and truer speech, — but as I live by bread, I doubt whether husbands and wives can keep that track together. You are a young Galahad with Lancelot's heart. I believe in you, I care mightily for you in a certain way; but you are a man, and none of the weaknesses of mankind are foreign to you. I am a woman, and, hard as my heart may be, it is made to be broken. Therefore say no more to me about this foolish fever of your youth. Believe me, it is a malady incident to the time. It will pass, in this present form, sometime to be renewed. You will love other women, and one day the unexpressive she will appear who has never once peeped into these worldly text-books. Hand in hand, she and you will learn the lesson together. It may be bitter, it may not. There are those, I believe, whom the gods forget; but I have no faith in myself escaping their thrusts.

THE DAY OF HIS YOUTH

Francis Hume to Zoe Montrose

WHY would you not let me talk to you yesterday, without waiting to depend on this poverty-stricken expedient? I have not had an instant alone with you. But I love you! I love you! Who shall prevent me from saying that! You may refuse to hear it, you may leave my letters unread; yet all the trees of the forest shall whisper it with gossiping tongues. But no more of this now. Your letter has made me feel imperatively that a demand has been made upon me: the demand of proving myself a man, and worthy, if any man can be, of the inestimable treasure of your heart. So it becomes me to be calm, and reply to what you say, not with mad protest, but with just consideration. I am a man, and no weakness of mankind is foreign to me. I grant it. (Though my heart throbs within me to swear such fealty as you have never yet dreamed. But let that pass. My life shall show.) Well, and suppose the first glow of new acquaintanceship does fade. Let it go. Might not something finer usurp its place, as the flower is more than leaf or bud? If it be possible that this great rapture should vanish (O, I know better than you, with all your worldly lore! It is perennial, ever-returning like the spring, though snows may intervene), do you think my tenderness would allow one sweet observance to fade? What infinite loving must grow of a daily life together, what fine consideration, what pride in each other's achievement, what mutual joy! I have talked long enough on paper. Take me, and let me serve you all my life, guard you, cherish you, and prove the truth.

Zoe Montrose to Francis Hume

TENDERNESS and constancy! that, my child, is friendship — it is not love. And I can gather a very good article of friendship from many a wayside bush without going over hot ploughshares

THE DAY OF HIS YOUTH

to seek it. Listen, and I will tell you exactly how I learned to interpret the later course of passion. I lived and breathed it side by side and heart to heart with a woman once. I will not tell you her name; she is living, and some time you may know her. I had a friend, and I loved her. She married a man who worshiped her, who was intoxicated by her as you are by me. He was her slave, if I may say that of one who took more than he bestowed; but though he absorbed her life and narrowed it in certain ways, he made her divinely happy. So it went on for years, until suddenly, through some new combination of circumstances, they were separated for a time, and he woke up. O telltale phrase in the life of a man! You don't know how much it means now, but you will know. She was dazed, confounded. Not that he was unkind to her; he was a gentleman, though a gentleman grown indifferent. About that time he drifted into friendship with another woman, led thereto, he would have said, by their kindred tastes. Nothing vicious here, nothing to distress the taste of law-abiding citizens; but a tragedy of the soul. I wonder if I can paint it for you. Here was a passionately devoted wife, taught by every act and word and look of years to depend for happiness on one living creature: to turn to him, as to the sun, for life and nourishment. Suddenly the sun was withdrawn, the light went out; she was expected to see by candle. Do not imagine that she betrayed him to me; we are not like that. I knew because she was so dear to me, and I had lived beside her and learned her thoughts. I felt the tragedy as it was enacted, day by day. I saw her poor face sodden with weeping. I suppose she reproached him at first, wildly, in woman's way. I suppose that because I knew him to be angry and bored. But when she saw little winning attentions which had once been hers given to another, I think it began to dawn upon her that they had never meant anything from the first. They were subjective, if I may put it so: a part of the man's nature, the trophy of any one who knew the password. Then the whole woman hardened. She reproached him no more. If he showered on her some of the unspent coin of his affection, she took it graciously, not treasuring it even in thought; because she dared not build again a house upon the sand. Her individuality grew mightily meantime. She became a creature of a wonderful strength and depth of thought; but her heart is dead within her. Sometimes I can see that she is even amused, in a pathetic way, at finding how lightly his indifference can pass over her. Now this was a good man, as men go. He would have scorned a sin larger than this romantic peccadillo, — but he was a man! He had waked up and found himself bored. And so would you! So far as I have been able to unravel it, what we call love is only a compound of selfishness and vanity. The lover gives so long as the return amuses him. He buys with his devotion a counter-devotion calculated to make him supremely happy; but when the story grows old, he yawns and goes elsewhere, either to smoke, run for office, write a book, or worship another woman. Never imagine that I decry men and exalt my own poor kind. Woman is the more constant only because she has been taught, through nature and inheritance, to give once and forever; and God made man to be gregarious.

I have told you my friend's secret. Now I will tell you mine. There is a man in the world — not you — who holds for me the fascination we are accustomed to call love. God knows, it is an earth-born attraction, for he is one who loves himself far more than he even professes to love me, and there is not one higher aspiration of my soul to which he would minister. He would tire of me, and he would break my heart. Therefore I will have none of him, though a mighty hand seems ever dragging me toward him, and though that part of me which is in love with the intoxications of life bids me make one throw for happiness and then die in despair. And neither will I have aught of you, though you seem to me a young St. Michael with lance of honor and shield of strength.

Francis Hume to Zoe Montrose

I DO not know why, but for some reason your letter has not killed my hope. Perhaps it would have done so, but I took it into the woods, the deeper woods, where I have begun to go of late to be wholly alone. For now even the tents by daylight seem to me like multitudes of eyes, and my father, also, breaks in on my dream. So I carried it to the woods where the light flickered and the shadows of little leaves played upon their larger mates. They seemed to me like the phantasmagoria of being. I had not begun to think of such things till I saw you. Life has grown infinitely sad, as well as infinitely beautiful. It has a haze: the haze of twilight. Well, the letter! It jarred upon me; that is a matter of course. It removed you from me, immeasurably, with its hints of a knowledge which I may never attain. When shall I be your equal, even in the wisdom of this world? You have known so many people; I only one. That of itself makes me sad. And then when I came to the inexplicable fact that there was one you might love, I felt within me a savage pain, a rising of hot blood, such as I never knew. What was it? Has it a name? Does it mean a futile passion because life, destiny, have treated us so brutally, setting you there and me here, so that your loves grew away from me, and the tendrils of your nature twined another way? And thus I sat suffering. But soon the wood drew me into her arms. I have never thought much about beauty; it has always been about me. But of late it has spoken with a new voice. O the quivering of the blue sky-patches, the duskiness of shade! The tree-trunks were black from the morning rain, and everything set upon a stem waved and fluttered, though so slightly that it was rhythm and not motion. The faint shadow on the tiarella leaf seemed to me divine; the maidenhair rustled greenly, and far off, in other arches, the thrush smote softly on his silver bells. And you were the soul of it. I should not have been surprised to see you there in some dim vista, with the sun upon your hair. But I shall never be surprised again at seeing you. You are in my world now; and my world cannot move without you. O, but I wish you were not so wise! I would you had never learned this strange and intricate game they call society. What profit is in it for you, but what infinite pain is there in it to me! These are the ironies of Those Who are above us. (That is my father's phrase; he talks of Them sometimes, in the night when he cannot sleep, and walks up and down the cabin as if he wished it were a world for width. The ironies of the immortal gods! I begin to understand my father a little now. I thought I understood him before.) We two, you and I, should have been born like twin birds in a nest, and gone singing away to the south. (Yet O my bird of the shining wing, O my bird! I would not have you other than you are.) We should have grown together, twin plants, from the sweet black earth, to twine and blossom and die. But it was not so to be; and therein I see what they call the hardships of life, and against such will I take my lance and shield, and ride forth. I will watch beside my arms, and draw down holiness from heaven, to be worthy to fight for you, and wear your favor. Not worthy of winning you — O, mistake me not in that! No heart was ever humbler than mine before its lady. Yet, as I am a man, my reward must come. I will win the world's delight, and I will wear her in the eye of the world: I, her plain and humble squire, whose only pride is to keep unsmirched for her fair sake. I have not your wisdom, but I begin to believe that I have a will to conquer; and it shall be bent upon my quest as if the world, — aye, and the sun! — were made for that. But tell me, you who know the lore of men, when we really begin to live, do we always ache so at the heart?

MY CHILD, — Your questions are delicious. What you felt on reading my letter? Yes, Sir Innocence, it hath a name: Jealousy. 'T is a very legitimate passion, so I think, but it hath earned in the world a bad repute. You white-armored child! this meeting a soul so dense to its own emotions is like cooling

Zoe Montrose to Francis Hume

drink in a desert. You complain because I am your senior and a trifle world-worn, and you do not know that you are complaining. You wish we had been born at the same minute. Pretty! poetic! but in plain prose, "I would you were not my elder!" And so would I; for if I were set back those five years, it would give me just five years more to hack away at my plays. I will not say how your moonings and mouthings would affect me; possibly then I might be caught by such pretty sweets. The last question of all: Does the world feel immortal pain at its heart? Frankly, yes. Nobody can be really happy except imbeciles and children; and not they, if they chance to be underfed. But be of good cheer. Only women ache all their lives long, every day of every year. They are an unintelligent lot, not to have learned self-protection. They wear their souls outside; and not being in the least original, they have not yet invented a thoroughly satisfactory coat of mail. For you, belonging to the lords of the earth, there will, after a time, be immunity. You will break your heart. (O, how infinitely wearisome to reflect that you have determined to break it about me!) Then you will waken to a vapid interest in work, discover your own nice talent for manipulating words, put all your past woes into verse, and by the time your reputation is made, you won't despise a good cigar and a club dinner. Nature has provided you as she has the lobster. Never fear; your claws will grow, though they may be often nipped. It is plain that you are to suffer, but I don't very much pity you. Unless you take to drink or any other unhygienic habit, you are sure to get something out of life. If you riddle your nerves, I won't answer for you. But, at the present moment, one thing must be done. Your letters must simply cease to be drenched with the night-dew of flimsy sentiment. Wring it out, and send them dry. Otherwise you get no answers. Do you hear, you gentle barbarian?

And I don't like your style overmuch. It isn't improving as I hoped. You don't want to drag out long, saccharine sentences, dripping with sugar as they crawl. Tell something! Let it be real, — or let it not be at all.

Francis Hume to Zoe Montrose

O THE irony stamped on those four little letters! Real! And my whole heart in it, a man's whole heart. That means something. But I obey you. Last night I dreamed all night long, one picture after another. First came this: I stood upon a dusty way, and multitudes of people were passing. They looked like you and like my father, but they were sad. They were bowed down, and many of them carried great brown bundles on their backs, bundles of wood, it seemed to me, or withered grass. Then I, too, grew very sad and heavy because every one else

THE DAY OF HIS YOUTH

seemed so; but suddenly my eye fell on a great light, and I wondered that I had not seen it before, and that none of them saw it. There, in the midst, by the roadside, stood the Apollo, warm, rosy, afire with life. His mantle was purple touched with rose: such color as we see in the east before the sun comes, and in the west after he is gone. His hair was long, and ran down his back in a great tawny river, — darker than yours, — and he stretched out his arm fearlessly holding the bow. Yet no one saw him but me. I fancied, even in my dream, that the arrow he would shoot might teach them a happier way to travel; but no one even knew he was there, or heard the twanging of the string or saw the cleaving of the arrow's flight. Then I sank down into darkness like a gulf, and only rose again to the splendor of another dream. The world seemed very large, larger than it does when you stand on the peak of Lone Mountain, with not a shade to cover you.

THE DAY OF HIS YOUTH

There were many people, in an agony of terror and pain, as Pierre was the night after I found him wounded and delirious from his fight with the bears. The people were old, and poor, and shabby, but still they looked like you, and their agony was dreadful to behold. They were all gazing upward, and I, too, turned my eyes to see, and lo! the heavens were all burning and brazen, and I saw that the heat was greater than I could endure. The sorrow and fear of those about me grew more terrible; they wept and wrung their hands, — still like Pierre, when he imagined he was again pursued. One thought came over me; and it seemed to me more awful than anything I saw. The trees! the sweet, faithful trees in all their newest green. They would be burned too. There would be no more sunrise or sunset. This was the last day of all, and not only should we burn, but so, too, would the little tender leaves. I dropped on my face, and kept saying softly — for it seemed as if One heard as much as if I cried aloud — "Mighty One, save the trees, only save the trees!" I did not know to whom I spoke, but I kept on saying it into the hot earth; and presently I heard a great shout from the throats of all the people. I rose slowly to my knees, to my feet, and everybody was laughing and throwing their arms about in joy. Still they were looking up, and I looked, too; and there, in the midst of the burning sky, was one little cool, clear patch of blue, as large as a maple leaf, and it was spreading fast. A fresh wind sprang up and blew from the west; and as the blue spread, little white clouds arose and danced over it. Even before we could get used to so great a bliss, the heaven was all blue and fleecy-winged, and the happy trees rustled greenly.

Again I dropped adown that darkling sea of death in life, and rose up again to find myself in a boat, floating, floating, on the wavelike ripples of a larger lake. So I knew it was the sea. I was near the shore, but yet not going in; and as I turned my eyes that way, I saw a height overhung with sky so blue! I have never seen such sky. But beneath and built upon the height was something more radiant than the sky itself: a temple with a wilderness of columns and vistas of columned shade within. The temple was of marble, mellowed and creamy, and rosy also, from some inner light, it seemed to me: something that glowed perennially and generated beauty as it glowed. And as I looked, wonder-stricken and alive with pure delight, one of the columns melted into air, and in the larger space it gave, stood you, my lady, clothed in white falling in folds more wonderful than the whorling of a bud within its sheath. You held a cup, and reached it to me with a smile divinely kind. I rose and plunged; the water closed over me, and sleep enwrapped me over.

THE DAY OF HIS YOUTH

And then again I rose, and I knew I was in Paradise; for it was a sunny forest of newly-budded trees, and I heard strange music and knew you would be with me soon and that all would be infinitely well with us forever. I sank back into measureless peace, the perfect patience of waiting. As I lay there, one came toward me, and although I could not see his face, I knew, this is an angel! He asked me some question, — what, I cannot tell; but I was in love with my pleasure of mind, and told him what was only half true. (You know they were talking of truth and lies at the camp the other night, and I was puzzled. Now I know what it is to tell a half-truth.) But as I spoke, the leaves of the trees withered and fell, and the birds left their contented harmony and began screaming in discord. The angel was gone, and I knew that heaven was destroyed, and I had done it. I woke, grasping my arms so tightly with either hand that the pressure hurt. I was sobbing for breath. But I was alive, and my heaven lay yet before me.

Have I done well? Here have I written you page upon page, only to earn a letter in return, when I long to fill these sheets with hot protestations, with petitions for your gentle ruth. At first it was enough to love you. At first? for the instant of recognizing my royal destiny; but now I would have all. Love me! love me! my heart cries and cries, for unless you know me for your own, what shall hinder me from losing you in this whirling progress of the days. You will go away; I heard them talking about it this morning. What am I to do then, I ask you? What am I to do? Mateless, solitary, left in the nest I was so long in building, while you fly south, the sun upon your shining wings. *What am I to do?*

THE DAY OF HIS YOUTH

YOUR last letter pleased me very well, all save its note of melancholy. Byronism is out of fashion. It isn't vendible, or it won't be in a few years, mark my words. In the time that is coming, men-children will rise up in literature and slash and slay and troll out hearty songs, born in the childhood of the race, and tell us of the love of woman, and the joy of martial blows. No more splitting of psychological hairs! The reaction is coming, and I thank the gods who make for us to mar. Moreover, you were hysterical at the end. Reform it altogether. No woman of any sense of humor was ever won by tears in the man who should be fighting for her. Take Tristram of Brittany for your model, not some laddie who should be in petticoats. Else you will never win fair lady. I speak generally, for it is understood from the start that this specific fair lady is not to be won at all. Woo her you may, so

Zoe Montrose to Francis Hume

THE DAY OF HIS YOUTH

you do it amusingly, robustly, with no whining like a hungry dog. She has little heart for "crumbling the hounds their messes." Now to business. I lay my commands upon you. A visitor is coming to camp: a man. While he is here, I shall have no time either to write or read, and I shall not visit the hollow tree. Moreover, you, as you be loyal and true, are to treat him fairly and kindly. If you hate my tendance of him as a stranger and a guest, you are to be only the more courteous. In short, as a knight peerless, you are to suffer manfully and in silence. For in silence lies the only true dignity left us by the chances of life. You see I own at once that you will suffer. That is inevitable; but I ask you to take the screw like a gentleman. There is no better word yet made.

THE DAY OF HIS YOUTH

To the Unknown Friend

I AM forbidden to write her. I must speak to some one, to something. He came three days ago. He is tall, black-eyed, with a laugh that rings. When I hear that laugh, I cannot even moisten my dry tongue. I have learned the meaning of hate. Yesterday she ran to the spring to bring him a glass of water. (He lay lazily and let her.) I followed.

"Is that the man you said you might love?" I whispered.

It looked as if the whisper burned her cheek. She turned red to the roots of her yellow hair. She could not look at me.

"Sir Knight," she said at last, "in the world we do not ask such things."

So I knew.

As to my manner, I think I have obeyed her. At least, I have been silent. But if this is to be my portion, death must come soon. For all my body is under the sway of this great trouble. I cannot eat. My hands seem helpless, they are so cold. My throat is choked. When have I slept? I think my father knows, and, though I cannot speak to him, understands, if a man for whom life is over can ever understand one at the beginning. Yet how can he? how can he? For my mother loved him, and gave herself to him. There is in all the world no sorrow like this of mine. To stand by and see another man help her into the boat and row away! To see him pin a flower in her hair with those daring hands! And I would have died to do it. Yet last night, as I stormed through the forest like the north wind that hates the clinging leaves, blind in the darkness, blind from within, — and only through some forest instinct keeping myself from crashing into tree and bush, — a moment of calm enwrapped me as quickly as if a gossamer veil had fallen from above. I seemed to see the meaning of things, the true meaning and value. That he should give her a flower, should take her hand, should win her smile — nay, the touch of her cheek, her lips — words I can scarcely write, even here, — what are these perishable gifts? Gauds of time! Did some poet say that, or have I made the phrase? The foolish broidery on the web of life, to wear and wear with years! But what lies behind to engender the token — ah, that is the eternal! I cannot penetrate her heart to see the living thoughts that thus denote themselves; but I know my own. I challenge time itself to match them with a brood more great. My love, my faith in her, my sacrifice, these are giants, springing into sudden Titanic birth, and Homer's heroes are pygmies to them. So the night calmed me, and I thanked God (did I ever write that word before? Did I ever really think it?) that my soul was born. But in the morning the mood had passed. I knew still what I had learned, but I could not feel it. My father, my dear father! He sits all

THE DAY OF HIS YOUTH

day with Homer open on his knee, and does not read. Once after the others had been here, and he saw me wince when she and the man went laughing off together, he said to me, almost as if he were afraid to say it: —

"Don't overestimate the little familiarities of social life." He said it, but I could not answer.

Zoe Montrose to Francis Hume

WELL — child! (You are nothing more — nothing!) Our guest has gone. Now let us hope you will straightway begin to get back your color. You look like the travesty of Hope Deferred. Dress you for Pierrot, and you'd serve well for the ghost of youthful folly. But you have behaved excellently. Socially speaking, you have watched beside your arms. Consider yourself knighted. Shall I tell you a secret? The Forest of Arden is not a proper trysting-place for folk who have met in the town; at least, if one of

THE DAY OF HIS YOUTH

them has been learning the sweet directness of the woods. For I, whom this man somewhat enchains and always did, — when I saw him among the trees, I knew he was very worldly and a trifle fat! And he does not swim well. And he slept o' mornings, and I could not help thinking of you wandering — albeit like a zany whose bauble is hid — in the dewy brake. Understand plainly, you are at this moment dear to me. The thought of you is sweet as Endymion to Diana; yet I who am no Dian, but a poor *fin de siècle* spinster, her being distorted by culture, would withdraw from you were you here, as the chaste huntress from Actæon. I like you; but I mean nothing by the saying, nothing, nothing! Nay, an I said "I love," it would be but lightly, as if we were both in a little play: a play which nobody wrote, and no man saw acted, and which the actors themselves will speedily forget. Think of the thistledowniest thing you ever saw, the most fleeting: the glow that rises in the sunset sky and flees before the sight. That is what I mean when I say you are dear to me. Do not make me repent having said it.

Francis Hume to Zoe Montrose

JUNE was it, June, sweet mistress of the
    changing year,
  (She of the brow serene, unpressed by
    cypress fear,
Nor darkened under bitter bud and leaf
By earth's old travail and the gray world's
    grief, —
Delighted by her changeful diadem
And fringed with roses round her mantle
    hem,)
Who laid thy hand in mine,
And said, with voice divine,
Like low-toned winds that wander to and fro
Searching out reedy pipes wherein to blow:
" This is your sacrament.
Drink ye, and be content.
This is life's flowering.
Now are ye queen and king."

THE DAY OF HIS YOUTH

O thought too poor and pale!
O words that wanly fail
For godlike Love's divine expressing,
And all the rhythm of his sweet confessing,
Whose full-voiced cry should be
Harmonious ecstasy.

Now are ye rulers of the upper air;
And though men surge below, not one shall dare
To scale the summit of your mystic height,
Nor breathe your breath, nor face your burning light.
The seed shall break for you, the seasons pass,
And you, serene, shall view as in a glass
The moving pageant of the happy year,
Fleeting from naked twig and garment sere,
To wrap itself in snows, to dream and dream
On budding boughs, and all the elusive gleam
Of happy rivers kissed
By sweet, bewildering mist.
And so to dream again, and rise in power
To the full glory of a new birth-hour.

THE DAY OF HIS YOUTH

The earth is thine, the starry spaces even,
The hour is thine, and maketh its own
    heaven —

I to write a marriage song, I! Shall mortal man hymn worthily his own love? Yet here is the initial note, the first faint stammering. Remember this, my love, my lady, my soul, — if I had known what your consent would be, I could never have waited for it all these years, here in the still woods. I should have died of hunger. Think of it! one only can bring bread for me, one only give me to drink. Be merciful to me, my bread-giver! One word — not on paper! One minute — let me see you alone!

Zoe Montrose to Francis Hume

DO not write verse until you fail to express yourself in prose. Verse should glide full-winged over the surface of the waters where the spirit of God lies sleeping. It should deal carelessly with poor things like prepositions and pronouns. They are but the spray-bubbles beaten back by its wings. Your smaller words are staffs falling as regularly and heavily as a tread on a board walk. Your phrases march; they do not fly. You will say that these lines were written under a pressure of strong emotion; but that's no reason. So might a prosy divine put forth his religion as an excuse for prosing. Have your emotion, but keep it to yourself if you can express it no better than this. It is neither "*magnifique*," nor is it — literature. Nor does your prose entirely please me. Look how it is tinged with its own sweetness. Everything is superlative. You are not content to say a thing in one way; you must say it in three, and then overload it with metaphor till the understanding balks at it. You write like this: —

"The night burned clear, illumined by a million stars. Memory was with me, and love; they, the divine. I was restless; I could not sleep. I came out of my chamber, impatient, praying for dawn."

Your images hunt in couples, and it won't do, save in the Psalms. Simplicity, simplicity! that must be our aim. That makes a sentence read as if it had stood immemorially, as if it formed an integral part of the Creator's speech when He overlooked His work and found it good. (You see I fall into your trick of repeated images. Indeed, it is one of the queer coincidences of fate that our phrasing should be much alike.) This same simplicity it is which shall make Ruskin a monument of white, like an angel with carven wings, when Sartor Resartus lies howling, with none so poor to patch him. Ah! and by the way — very much by the way — don't be feverish again. Don't take my idle words of last time for more than they are worth. I told you they meant nothing. When will you believe?

THE DAY OF HIS YOUTH

THEIR nothing is my all. You have declared it. The words lie in my hand. Discourse to a man upon rhetoric, when your own letter says, "You are dear to me"! We will talk this out. We will, I say. If not alone, before them all. Come into the woods with me to-night at nine, and with only the dark for witness you shall swear to me love — or denial.

Francis Hume to Zoe Montrose

WAS it a week ago we spoke together there by the rock, and have you changed me so? I told you that night I half thought — I was very sure — I cared, and then I seemed to lose my power of mocking you. Our places are changed. You do not know it, but I no longer command; I am beginning, the real I that sits within me, to obey. Your ways are so sweet, so tender, your truth so single, your chivalry so great!

Zoe Montrose to Francis Hume

THE DAY OF HIS YOUTH

I am learning to lean on your fair service as it were an arm. O, but if I am to love you, make me good! I wish I were what you would have me be. I am not! I am not! How soon will you learn it? They talk about a maiden's mind, a fair white page; mine is all tracked with ugly marks. I am blonde, young, pretty, but I am haggard and yellow within. Not bad, you know, dear; but not the she you should have loved. Full of worldliness, cynicism, incapacity for being deceived; there's not a spontaneous thing about me. Yet, peradventure, my only hope is that I see your beauty and love it. No more of this, so long as we two live. Love me while you can, and believe it is my unhappiness that I have lived too much.

Francis Hume to Zoe Montrose

MY LADY, — It was a perverse mood that conceived your letter. And if you had no perversity, no pretty whims, where should we all be? On a dead level of discontent. I love the sweet humility of it. Not that I would have you keep to that; it would never befit my sovereign lady. But for an idle moment of a summer's day, 't is like fooling in masquerade. Why, you are queen of me, and queen of my great heart! (Aye, I do swear with the biggest oaths I know that 't is a great heart; for otherwise were to do you some despite. Did you not create it? "Let there be love," said you, and straightway my heart was born.) Do people always take it so seriously when other people say they are going to marry? What was that unguarded speech of Mrs. Montrose's : —

"Zoe, Zoe, why did n't you let that boy alone?"

O, I heard it, but I forgive her! She wots not of our kingdom. What should a woman with false hair and fat hands know about the divine foreknowledge of a heart in finding its mate? And my father? Why is he sadder every day? He has not lost me. He had gained you; and he owns you are sweet and blithe and fair beyond compare.

Later: What do you think has happened? I am to go back with you, and my father himself proposed it! I could wake all the echoes in the hills with joy. I shall never walk any more. I shall run and dance. What will your world think of that, — your world of men and women? Even that my father takes it sadly does not move me overmuch, though I wish he saw the joy of being. (How full it is, O, how full! And you have brought me the cup. I will drink carefully, sweetheart, though so greedily. I will not spill a drop.) He said to me, "You must know something of life before you make new ties and take responsibilities. So you must go out into the world. Mrs. Montrose is a good woman. She will be your teacher in social walks, and she will introduce you to some men

THE DAY OF HIS YOUTH

I knew long ago. I can't give you definite plans. You would n't follow them if I did." When I asked him if he would go, too, he said, "No, not yet." It was best for me to cut loose from him for a time.

So, fine sweetheart! I am going back with you to your city. We are not to be separated for a single day: perhaps not until the hour when you stand up before your people and swear to cleave to me only. I read that service yesterday, alone in the woods. Gods! how great it is! and yet not great enough. I would not have it "till death." It should cover the abyss — and hell. Do you remember to think with every breath you draw how a man loves you? how he would fain have you *his* breath, that he might draw you into his very veins? Ah, what words are there for the telling? How poverty-stricken are we that there should be no way to make you mine save by swearing oaths! If I could give you my blood —

but even that is less dear to me than one instant in your presence. If I could sacrifice the dearest thing I have — yet that would not be life itself; it would be you. Sacrifice you to love, to prove I love you! What wisdom were in that?

Zoe Montrose to Francis Hume

DEAR, — Step back before it is too late. Do not come with us. No good lies that way. Why should you leave your happy island for the grimy streets? There is strange irony, too, in your setting off with us, such wayworn travelers. So might a spangled troup of weary players entice a sleepy child that had only known the lambs and birds, and lain on fragrant hay, to take some part in their ghastly mummery. What should be his fate? footsore, bewildered, to fall beside a wayside ditch, and gasp his breath out in the dusty fern. Go back! I'll none of you. I won't take the responsibility of your shining soul. Stay here, and

THE DAY OF HIS YOUTH

write the story of your island. Tell the weary old world what the leaves whisper and how the flower-buds open. And folks will smile the vacuous smile of ignorant criticism, and say, "O, yes, we all knew it before!" Then perhaps your Virginia will come, and you may die in each other's arms. For you have n't the fortunate palm, my boy; you have n't the look of luck. They that make us have ordained you to grief, and I would for forty shillings that your slaughter came not through me. I will go to town. You shall send me your manuscripts, I will find a publisher, and we will write each other letters — so friendly, so friendly — and when you die with Virginia I will come to the woods and sit by your grave, and sing you little songs in remembrance of the love that was not to be mine. So fare you well; and I wish you only forgetfulness.

THE DAY OF HIS YOUTH

Francis Hume to Zoe Montrose

FAREWELL! I stop in my packing to laugh. I've begun to sing the word, to whistle little tunes to its rhythm. Aye, mistress, we will fare well, but we fare together! It has just occurred to me that my packing is very queer indeed: violin, gun, my few dearest books, and almost no clothes. For my father says camp clothes, however new, won't wear the air of town, and my tailor must be my first friend. Farewell, indeed! Can you toss a bridegroom a two-syllabled word over your shoulder, and turn him back at the door of the church? What is a church like? Is it true the aisles are forest vistas? So the books say. O, the great race of men, to have put nature into wood and stone!

THE DAY OF HIS YOUTH

THE TREMONT HOUSE, BOSTON.

Francis Hume to Ernest Hume

I AM here, exactly where you told me to go, though Mrs. Montrose asked me very cordially, again and again, to make my home with her. In front of the hotel is a noisy, rattling street, full of madness, clamor, and delight. (I said this to Zoe, and she laughed herself faint. "Intoxicated by a Boston street!" said she. "Wait till you see Paris.") At the side of the hotel is a yard full of graves, with little stones, row upon row. O, so many graves! I realize what multitudes of men have died, and how old the world must be. I thought of it last night, and it bore upon me so, grave upon grave — and all the unnumbered dead of all the wars — and I rose to look from my window into the busy, lighted night, and think of men. How they seethe here in crowds. How they hurry up and down, each in his little world, king of that alone, and alien to his brother. It is so strange. I think I should die of loneliness if I had not brought my own with me. But does any one sleep? There is no air!

O father, why are you not here! We went to the theatre to see a woman — I told you we were going. I never so longed for speech. If only I might describe her, even half worthily! I send you a package of photographs, all I can find, but they stammer and halt as I do. First, she is tall, very tall, I think, and there is in her a strange mingling of angularity and the divinest grace. She seems to have members like another, but the most perfect genius and harmony in the use of them. Her hand is gracious, large; it has not that subtile outline of Zoe's, but she uses it as an instrument potent for beauty. Her head is not set proudly, her shoulders are not like the pine-tree, and Mrs. Montrose tells me her clothes are wrinkled and sometimes frayed at the seams. But her face! All the Graces strove for mastery, and threw their gifts at her in a blind contention, so that none of them agree. They simply strive together like a company of angels, ill-assorted, and give you the effect of a lovely surprise. Her brows are full of pathos. Between them there is ever a little irregular frown; and her eyes look out beneath, imploring, piteous, saying, "I have lost my way. Will somebody tell me where to go?" And her mouth! O, the merriest mouth, made for joy, made for light words and blithest laughter! Her hair is dancing yellow, and she herself dances, her spirit most of all. I have felt joy, but I never saw it until now. Zoe laughs at me, and opens her eyes because I have begun to talk of good and bad, of beauty and ugliness. She says I am too apt. It is true that I have done little but study faces since I came. Many are like animals. Some I love; some I hate at once. I have seen three persons who are deformed, with humps on their backs. They have a strange old look, with a queer brightness in the eyes; and when I catch that look on those who are straight and well, I wonder if they are deformed in the soul. But whoever else is to be shrunk from, my player-lady is all-worthy. As I saw her fleet about the stage, buoyant in joy and then maddened by grief unspeakable, I did not see her alone. I caught glimpses of Shakespeare's women, for she had a trace of them all: Portia, full-winged for justice; Juliet, passion-doomed; Imogen, your love of loves; but most of all Beatrice, the iris-spirit, and Ophelia, piteously undone. Then I remembered, "A star danced," and hot tears burned my eyes. Father, how do we live when we feel so much? And the world, so great, so piercing in its beauty — how it presses upon us! Yet I suppose there must be a certain habit of inner control; for though it is beautiful to Zoe, she does not ache as I do. No, she laughs. I must get the habit of laughter. But you see I have been up all night, thinking of this woman and the world she opens to me; of her and the woman I love. Of Zoe I think always, father; but you know I could n't write that. No man could, could he?

... I have been to church. It is strangely disappointing. Of the church itself it is not necessary to speak. It seems there are no great cathedrals here; I had not realized that. The music was fine, but faint; I found I had expected not a quartette but a chorus, a multitude praising God. Then the clergyman spoke. It was very vague and very long. It seemed to me unnecessary for him to have written anything, when he might have read Emerson or Ruskin. I forgot him, after a time, and began to think of Lone Mountain and the rhythm of the wind over the firs. The sermon was something about St. John's visions and the church. It seemed to me belittling, as if a primer should be written to explain the gods.

But perhaps I have to get the habit of church-going also.

I have been introduced to dozens of people. Dozens? let me say hundreds. They are very kind. You ask me to speak frankly of civilized life. Frankly then, these people we meet in battalions I do not like. That is, I might like them individually if they appeared under a different system; but society seems to me an intricate sort of game which anybody could play, but which is very puzzling to the onlooker and not in the least worth learning. For example, their conversation: a great deal of it is mere personality, and they only speak of a certain set. That may be a truism. I have apparently said that they do not talk of the people they do not know because they only talk of the people they know. But I find there are such different ways of talking. People seem to be in groups, and each group is labeled. I am in the smart set! I fancy some of them consider the

THE DAY OF HIS YOUTH

persons who play and sing and write books (that is unless they don't do it particularly well) as a class of beings made for their amusement; and if it is necessary to speak of scientists or diplomats, they do it with a certain languid interest, and then put them aside in a drawer. There is a great deal of philanthropy, but it is not what I thought about love of man, when I read the old stories of the saints and those greater than saints who came to redeem. It does not look like love; for love draws one nearer, clasps its arms about one; is it not so? This is a kind of business appointed for certain days in the week, just as one attends church on Sunday. They "go down" to obscure streets and visit, and they even make reports afterwards; but it is something like the German lessons three times a week or the piano practice every day. But who am I to blame them? I have walked through the poorer streets. I have looked boldly into the

THE DAY OF HIS YOUTH

faces there, and, father, I hate them. I would not touch them for worlds, those deformed, dirty, ugly, loathsome creatures. They are so unbeautiful! And there surely can be no need of that. They might at least have the beauty of cleanliness and of lovely thoughts. Apparently I cannot get the habit of philanthropy, however well I may do with church-going. For how can we help being repulsed by what is repulsive? As well expect the bees to seek carrion instead of roses. But what do the books mean when they talk about love of men? The more men need love, the less one can love them. Write me, father. I feel as if I should know a different side of you through your letters.

Later: O, I am glad I came, if only for this one thing — a little cat, a little mangled cat, gaunt, wounded, dying. I killed her — mercifully.

DEAR FRIEND,—Only a word, to save my honor: for we lunch and tea and dine with the world to-day. Your barbarian is more than perfect. He has become a social sovereign, sweeping all before him; and he does n't even know it. He stands there in a circle of pretty girls and strenuous spinsters, looks at them gravely with those great soft eyes, answers their questions, and walks away in absolute unconsciousness. He says people are so kind. On the contrary, they are enraptured with his beauty and his miraculous truth-telling. And I begin to think Zoe may really be in love with him. If nobody interferes with them, perhaps they'll make a model Darby and Joan.

Mrs. Montrose to Ernest Hume

DEAR SON,—So you don't love the poor! Well, don't force it. They are not invariably beautiful. Don't trou-

Ernest Hume to Francis Hume

ble about them until you have found out why they haven't Greek profiles, as a rule, and why they sometimes fail in expressing their lovely thoughts. Why did the cat appeal to you? Yet she wasn't beautiful. Something had maimed her. That might be the case with two-legged creatures also. I have been thinking about you a lot. In fact, for the last twenty years there hasn't been anything else for me to think about, except what is gone. And that is a chapter by itself. But I want to tell you this: if you are in a tight place of any sort, moral or financial, come to me, and I shall be grateful. I'm older, and I have lived in the world. I don't want to be a prig and hamper you with moral maxims; but if you need me, I want to be there. Moreover, I want you to grapple alone with life. That's the only way. To catch systematically at another swimmer is to weaken yourself and perhaps go down, — as I did, though not for the same reason. I went

THE DAY OF HIS YOUTH

down because I never was a strong swimmer in the beginning, and then I did n't go in for training. Enough of metaphor. I've a sort of legacy, though, to give you. I was thinking last night what a shame it is that we never have a fair show with temptation, because a temptation is a thing that's never recognized until you see its back: like the hill-wives. But this you may remember; if something seems particularly enticing to you, and you say, "It would n't do for all the world to take this, but it will do for me," draw back. That is mirage. If you begin to shield yourself behind what the great souls have done, that, too, is mirage. The great souls are never so little as in forsaking law for license. Do not despise what convention has decreed, unless you know it to be trivial and false. The general consensus of mankind really means something. A hot-headed and hot-hearted youngling in revolt against harness is pretty sure to get a galled back — and nothing else. Pin yourself to law; only make sure that the law is the highest possible. So much for Polonius. Now, your legacy; and now I have to write things almost too sacred to be written, and that never could be said. I have always talked to you about your mother, because you have a right to know her; but her loss is so fresh, that every word still hurts. She was probably the most rounded, the purest, the most crystalline nature ever made. Her perfection could never have been exceeded. Perhaps Imogen only was her equal. Have you ever thought what it must have been to such a woman to conceive and bear a child? She loved me. Our life was as perfect as her desert. Now I know the thoughts — all she could tell even me — of that girl-mother every day of all the weeks before your birth. There is no word — at least from me — fine enough to describe the course of that holy rapture. There is in a woman's love a certain joy in the pain which is borne for love's sake, a certain ecstasy of renunciation which no man ever feels. That once I saw it pictured. I veil my face. She was not only divinely happy because you were coming; she became divinely holy. Her child seemed to be a sacrifice to present to God, — her God was very living, very near her, — and she had resolved that he should be a perfect gift. She heard the most beautiful music, and clothed herself in the finest fabrics. She had her room hung with angelic faces, where her eyes could open first upon them in the morning. Those are the pictures that hang in our cabin. I could never tell you why I chose them. Mona Lisa was banished, though she loved her, too. But she said, "He shall have the simplicity of God; he shall not bear the beauty of the world." She read the most wonderful books then, the simplest, the most exalted. I have tried to remember her choice among them, and it seems to me

THE DAY OF HIS YOUTH

now that she chose always what had the wisdom of truth and love, and that she shrank from the sparkling and clever. I cannot tell you all her thoughts about you, nor all her hopes. For, indeed, the confidences were mine, and near as you are to me, she is nearer. Perhaps I could never have told you if you had not begun to see what it is to love a woman. But the substance of it all seems to be this: she loved you before she saw you; she worshiped the very thought of your coming. She seemed to feel that she was not a passive instrument chosen to bring you into the world. (You see I speak personally now of the Unknowable. It is because she did so. To her, all the powers that fashion and rule were blended in One, and He was warm and living, and she loved Him. Yet her idea was not anthropomorphic. It was colossal. This was and is incomprehensible to me; but I am trying now to enter her habit of mind.) A passive instrument, did I write? She was, in a way, your creator. The vital spark came from her God through love and her, and she would not hamper it by any earthly clogs of groveling inheritance. Well — her watching upon her arms was over. She saw her son. And then she gave him to me to finish her work, and died. Now the knowledge of her great love and expectation seems to belong to you, and I have only this to say: If you feel yourself getting a little dusty in life, think what should be expected of one who was so loved, so waited for. You are of royal stock; for you were born of a woman so perfect that sometimes I wonder now if I have not imagined her. But I have not. She was real. We do not guess out things so beautiful. God — It — Nature — makes them, and then we describe them in verse or music, and people say we create. Don't speak to me of this; only make use of it when the time comes.

There is n't much to tell you about

camp. I do many of the same old things. Perhaps I shall go to you; for sometimes I think you will not want to come back. Pierre misses you.

To the Unknown Friend

I HATE vulgarity! Mrs. Montrose seems to be a very good woman, but she *is* vulgar. Why, when women are middle-aged and portly, do they feel at liberty to make rude personal speeches? She said to me yesterday: —

"If you want to marry Zoe, marry her soon." I was angry; I could only look at her. She laughed, but she did flush. "Don't glare at me, Ingomar," said she. "I'm speaking for your good. It is n't well for you to marry her, but somehow you're the kind of a child I want to see pleased. So keep on the spot. Captain Morton has come back, and he knows Zoe has had some money left her. Be on the spot!" I walked away without a word. Since then I have hardly seen Zoe. It is insulting to go near her. As if I did not trust her! As if I would be "on the spot!"

I CAN'T wait to tell you! so this *Zoe Mont-*
goes round to you by messenger. You *rose to*
could n't guess it out in a lifetime. I *Francis*
am rich, truly rich! Uncle Obed has *Hume*
died. He was a miser, God bless him! and he's left it all to me. Did you ever hear of anything so absurd? Now I can buy myself elegant leisure, as if it were something to be found at the shops. I can give myself time to write my plays. I can even bring them out. Of course, though I lead the horse to water I can't make him drink; and though I were Midas I can't force the public to listen. Stay! is it impossible? Go to! there shall be souvenir nights, and the newspapers shall be fully primed. Actresses shall pose as injured wives, and scandals shall be described in flaming headlines.

THE DAY OF HIS YOUTH

All print is open to us. We are rich, rich! I'm quite delirious with it.

Francis Hume to Zoe Montrose

LOVE, — You bewilder me. I did n't know you cared. Money? I did n't know you wanted it. I believe we have a great deal. My father told me I need not stint. Don't use yours. Please don't use it. Marry me to-morrow, and take mine.

Zoe Montrose to Francis Hume

DON'T use it? Why, I *want* to use it! You might as well ask a new-crowned king to go and make a visit in central Africa, and pick up all the gold he could carry. Be patient. I'll come to Africa by and by. But just now I want to take mine ease in the opulence of my mind. I'm having a new dress made of a queer dull green and blue, and I'll buy a set of turquoises, God wot, and present them to myself from my dearest friend. Uncle Obed lived and died in South America. I won't wear mourning—I won't! I won't! Perhaps green and blue are mourning there.

DEAREST LADY,—Will you write me—just a word, only a word? You see I could not get a whisper from you last night, and you were so brilliant and sparkling, like a shining gem. Call me a baby, if you like. I don't mind. Only say you love me. Just the three words, dear? And will you take these little blue stones? I can see how they would look against your skin; I held them near a pinkish rose, and then I saw you in my mind and I threw the rose aside. Dear, the three words? I feel very humble, very much of a beggar. Will you?

Francis Hume to Zoe Montrose

THE DAY OF HIS YOUTH

Zoe Montrose to Francis Hume

NOW you are not sleeping, as I said when I saw the hollows coming under your eyes, or you would n't fail in tact. It is n't like you. I want to buy my turquoises myself. Don't you see how I am luxuriating in the sense of unfamiliar power? It will pass, and then I'll take your gift. Of course — the three words — *of course;* but I can't be always writing them. They look so bathetic. Now I've seemed brutal and ill-tempered, all in one letter. But why will you be faultless and appealing, and why won't you see I am a child of the earth (the street-earth — paving-stones ground up and mixed with champagne) and go home to your birds and trees?

Zoe Montrose to Francis Hume

YOU were not interesting last night, and Captain Morton was; therefore I sat out with him. But you should not have turned white and frozen in a corner. That sort of docile remonstrance in you rouses my aunt to a height of righteousness which nature itself cannot endure. I mean my nature. She says you are perfection, and that I don't deserve you. The maxims are unimpeachable; I agree to both. Go, if you like, or stay and be agreeable. I forgot to tell you that I am going to New York to visit Alice May, Captain Morton's cousin. Auntie is angry. Are you angry, too? Is all the world suspicious, and of Othello's complexion? If the primitive passions do rage just as furiously even though we speak Victorian English, tell me, what's the use of development? We are simply more trammeled and less frank. Having blown off the steam of my wrath, I'll condescend to say that the invitation from Alice just reached me, and that I have decided quite suddenly. Again, does it make you angry? Would you rather have me fettered to your wrist by a nice, neat little chain with your monogram on it and a jeweled padlock?

Francis Hume to Zoe Montrose

ANGRY because you are going away? My lady, heart of me, you know me better. You are free from everything but my love. It follows you everywhere, poor pensioner. It has nothing to claim, nothing to exact. Give it place in your suite, and be patient with it; for it would hide away rather than break in upon your mood. All your moods are like crystal bubbles, no more to be shivered than one of God's beautiful worlds. I love you; but you are infinitely sacred, infinitely precious to me,—above all, and above measure, free. Go, dearest lady; be happy. Think of me when the thought is an added pleasure, and then—come back to me.

THE DAY OF HIS YOUTH

DEAR, — O, at moments like this I feel as if I could repay you so royally! You are a knight peerless. Remember, whatever comes between us, that I knew this of you. I shall always think of you with reverence. If you were here, perhaps I should be perverse and willful, and prick your offered hand with some tempestuous thorn; but I do meet you with one half my soul — perhaps with all my real soul. I send you a kiss. Come to the station if you like; but it will be to see the outer me, the worldly one.

Zoe Montrose to Francis Hume

SHE is gone. There is nothing to do for a week — a month, perhaps — but prowl about this dismal city, looking in the faces of men. At the theatres there is heavy comedy played by buffoons. So I stay away and watch my kind, and wonder what I'm going to do to make a

To the Unknown Friend

THE DAY OF HIS YOUTH

man of myself. Write? What? Worldfuls of thought are creating themselves within me, but as yet they are only stardust. I doubt if they will be anything more. There is a strange ache in my throat, a strange failing within me. Is it what children call homesickness? I heard little Ethel Wynne, the other day, talking about her first visit from home:

"They put me to bed, and I cried and cried all alone, and I was sick at my stomach, and *I pitied me.*"

"Poor Mother Bunch!" said her father. "Homesick!"

And I believe I "pity me," too. I must be a weak sort of a fellow. All the men I meet are absorbed in something — horse — college — games. I am sick for the unknown. Not the camp. I believe the loneliness there would kill me now. O, why talk of it, for the sole use of spending myself on paper! I am sick for her — her! Heavens — whatever that means — how terrible it is to love a woman! Yet it seems so simple. If she loved me — oh, she does love me, but she has her moods. She is compact of fire and air and dew, and her path is like the swallow's. How should I find her?

I AM taking violin lessons, as you suggest; also French. The verdict, in each case, is that I have been wonderfully well taught. I begin to know you for a genius. How have you managed to do so many things to perfection? The Frenchman, Dr. Pascal, is stirring my brain more than anything has yet succeeded in doing. So far I have felt like a muddy pool in which the stars and gas lamps try to reflect themselves and get only broken gleams in return. He is unsparingly critical of our American civilization, and feels at liberty to say so to me, because I am primeval man, fresh from my woods. He tells me such

Francis Hume to Ernest Hume

marvels of the French. According to him, they are the creators of form: form in art, in language, in mechanism. If I could reproduce his thought, it would be to tell you that, as we are the youngest of nations, so, too, are we the crudest. We are eaten up by an infinite complacency. Because we are big, we fancy we blot out the sun whenever we choose to turn our bulk. We submit to a thousand public abuses because we are too drenched in our own fatness to criticise or disturb ourselves. The individual is rampant, and all are enslaved. Consequently, this is not the land of liberty, but of license, overrun by a wild chase of "every man for himself." We worship our wealth, and not what it brings us. We adore display; it tickles us more to scatter money broadcast in blazonry than to live in chaste democracy and erect monuments to our public good. To beauty we are almost totally blind and deaf; and what wonder, when there is no *milieu!* We

THE DAY OF HIS YOUTH

do not breathe an æsthetic atmosphere. Our public buildings are atrocious, and — and — I could go on for pages, but I spare you. The worst of it is that it may be true. You know how much my opinion is worth. I might as well be a boy of ten for all I can say, judged by experience and comparison; but to me everything in this city is small, disappointing, unbeautiful. Nothing, except the music, fills my ideal of what I thought life would be when I pictured it in my tent. Is life small? Are men pygmies? Or are my judgments naught?

YOU are right in distrusting your judgments. I should not trust them, either, because, as you say, you have no standard of comparison. But I think this may truly be said. America is young, and therefore you must not expect of her a full artistic development. She has done some of the greatest moral

Ernest Hume to Francis Hume

work imaginable. There her instinct was unspoiled, just as that of youth should be. She came "trailing clouds of glory." But art is not the flower of the moment. Neither is it to be borrowed from other lands; though thus may we obtain the technique which teaches appreciation. A few geniuses seem to be born full-fledged; I doubt if a nation could be. A man, even a genius, has to learn to use his tools. So does a people. The French are form-mad. I don't wonder. Outer beauty is a subtile poison. Once taste it and you never lose the craving. It is a beautiful zeal, but not always the best zeal. I've been a coward and an absentee about life myself, but I'd rather trust some of those vigorous old pirates like Sir Francis Drake, who went about picking up new worlds like huckleberries, than a carpet-knight on tiptoe at the apex of civilization. But don't misunderstand me. My pen ran away. I don't undervalue your Frenchman. I only say, Be

THE DAY OF HIS YOUTH

patient with America. She is so young, poor girl! The only discouraging thing about it is, as he says, that she does n't know it. If she would learn of her grandams and great-aunts, she would burn her fingers and tear her frock less often. Her lovers must simply be patient and wait till she grows to her task. Perhaps when she really is older and stronger, and has lifted her straw a day, she 'll be capable of carrying this burden of government. No, she has n't solved her problem yet; democracy is the highest form of government, but she does not yet know how to administer it. I find I am not so far out of gear with civilization as I thought, for I have strong ambitions for you. I find I want you to take up the fardel of public life; not to be a pessimistic complainer, standing aside with your hands in your pockets, but a citizen. And if you can do something, too, for art — but after all, I shall be content if you keep your soul clean.

Zoe Montrose to Francis Hume

DEAR LADDIE, — I have a great deal to say to you, and I am utterly incapable of saying it. So the only resource I have is to be short and trust to your intuitions. You can supply my remorse, and my grief that life is what it is. We are blind instruments of blinder fate. Captain Morton came here soon after I did. You knew that. He says plainly that he came to see me. More than that, he came to see me because he loved me. If there is anything in love, is n't it this power of one creature over another? Are we responsible? Are we true to ourselves if we fight against it? I, at least, could not fight. If my bond to you had been a thousand times more strong, I should have snapped it like twine. I told him I would write you that it is broken. I wish life might be good to you, though I cannot be. And I wish I might never see you again, now, or after my marriage. I don't say, Forgive me. You can't yet, but some time perhaps you will.

DEAR LADY,— Since your letter reached me, I have written you a great many answers. None of them are worth sending. This is all I tried to say. You are just as much loved as before, and you are free,— perfectly, entirely free. It must be for you exactly as if you had never been bound. And you shall never see me.

Francis Hume to Zoe Montrose

THERE must be some outlet for this, or I shall be talking to people in the street. They will think I am crazy, and that will be the end of it. So I'll put it all down, madness and all. So Francis Hume came up to town, did he? And lost his love! He was well enough, poor fool, down in the woods; but the Great Ones that plague us for

To the Unknown Friend

their sport sent him a mirage, and it dazzled him, and he sailed after it. No! no! no! It was not mirage. It was true — a true, true vision. She is real, and sweet, and sound, my lady with the merry laugh and seeking eyes. I had her; I have the vision of her. I wish I did not remember such piercing lines: "My good days are over!" And poor Thekla, —

"Ich habe gelebt und geliebet."

Here's a supposition. Is a woman betrayed more lost than a man's soul when it is rejected and thrown back to live alone? Perhaps there is a difference. But this lonesomeness of the heart! If I died, should I still live and be I, bearing my wormwood with me? A life shattered so early! "You have broken my globe! you have broken my globe!"

They have come back to Boston, he and she. They came together, and I saw them. I watched him go up the

THE DAY OF HIS YOUTH

steps with her, and heard him laugh when they went in. I sat on a seat in the mall, and watched. He wears a strange significance for me. I suppose I hate him, really; and yet, because she loves him, he holds a new and awful interest. It is really as if *I* loved him. I think of him with her thoughts; how strong he is, how black those eyes, how white his hands, how round his voice. And every thought poisons me, and I roll in my nettles and sting myself deeper.

. . . I loved a woman — O God! betrayed! betrayed! Not by her. O God, save her from punishment and remorse! She was deceived. She shall not suffer.

. . . I do not know what God is. I sat thinking of Him an hour in the dark, last night. All I know is that mankind has made Him. He is the cry raised by their united voices when they wail. He is the uttermost anguish of their hearts. They had to call it something, this wail of terror and grief, and so they called it

God. I call it God, too. I lift up my voice with theirs, and cry, God! God!

... I have taken to following them about the town. They went to the theatre last night. I sat in the gallery, and looked down on them. How familiar she seems — how truly mine! Can anybody steal what is mine? After the theatre I slept a little, and dreamed that we were on a shore, a silver strip of sands, with the sea black before us. I dragged her from him, and when I had struck him down, she turned to me, with a glad, low cry, and clung to me, all warm. She was glad! And I have been warm about the heart all day, for the remembrance dwells with me. How beautiful it would be to kill him, if after it was all over she would turn to me and rest here in my arms!

Once I could have lived through this. There would have been horse and hound and battle-axe — sword and lance — all the rest of it. I could have gone away to the wars and worked off some of this horror. And now, like a rat in a trap, I've got to sit still here and go mad.

DEAR FRIEND,— We have made a wretched botch of it among us, with your poor boy. Zoe has jilted him. We might have guessed it. He has simply disappeared. He left a card here, and quietly changed his lodgings. At the Tremont House, they either don't know where he has gone or refuse to say. I am worried about him. Poor boy! poor boy! he won love everywhere, but he didn't want it. Only hers; and Captain Morton could have conjured her into a black cat any time these three years, if he had chosen. Don't blame me. There's a fate in things; and if you wanted your boy to escape tragedy, you shouldn't have given him that face.

Mrs. Montrose to Ernest Hume

THE DAY OF HIS YOUTH

Ernest Hume to Francis Hume

DEAR BOY,—Could you come down and see me a bit? I'm having a series of colds, and they keep me in bed and make me melancholy-stupid. Then, when you go back, perhaps I can go with you. Where are you now? From your giving the address of a post-office box, I fancy you have left the Tremont House. When will you come?

Francis Hume to Ernest Hume

DEAR FATHER,—I will come soon. I can't quite yet. I am sorry you are not well. I will come soon.

To the Unknown Friend

THE voices of people about me do hurt me so. I won't see a soul I know, but the waiters asking for orders —O, they hurt me so! I shall be like a woman, and scream. I can't see my father yet—not yet. I could n't bear his face, or his voice. They would be so kind. I must be alone. Yet it is awful for crazy people to be alone. They are so beset by dreams — and faces. I don't think they are real, but still there are faces.

. . . My God! what have I seen to-day! I went walking — fast, fast — and I took the poorest streets, so that I might not meet any one I know. And all the animal-people — hog, rabbit, fox, cat, and the rest — kept coming toward me as I walked; for now there seems to be a sort of mist in the air, and one face flares out of the mist and then another. And it rushed over me suddenly how they must ache and suffer and languish to be so poor and so ignorant and vile. There is a dropping inside my heart, all the time, as if the blood that ought to nourish me were falling and falling and wasting itself in pain. And I began to look into the faces, and it seemed to me as if these people, too, were all of them bleeding. The ground was red and soaked. And then I learned that all this great world is in pain just like my own. I did not seem so much alone then — not quite. They were like me, all of them. I began to see how some might love them; and the more hideous they were, so much the more could one love. *Who was Jesus Christ?*

. . . I went to the Passion Music, and sat alone in a little crowded corner, afraid of being seen. It crucified my soul. I felt as if the violins were bowing on my brain, sawing the little gray strings that are my nerves. And then it came upon me like an overwhelming sea. This Man — this God-man — loved the whole world and was rejected by it. I loved one; and because she cast me off, I am as I am. True or not — His story — but *is* it true?

. . . Yet I cannot stop loving her. I love her to-day more, more, a thousand times more, if that can be. Is it true I have no right to love her? Then I have no right to breathe. I had no right to be born.

DEAR FRANCIS, — Won't you come down for a day or two? If not, I think I shall go to you. Write me a word. *Ernest Hume to Francis Hume*

DEAR FATHER, — Try to be patient with me. I'll come soon, truly soon. I'm not very good company. I'm thinking things out. *Francis Hume to Ernest Hume*

CONCORD, N. H.

ERNEST HUME sick here with pneumonia. Come. *Telegram to Francis Hume*

I AM glad you got off so well, and that the sun shone at last. Ever so many presents have come since you left. Mrs. Badger sends a Turkish rug, hid- *Mrs. Montrose to Zoe Morton* eous, I think, and abominably dirty. I smelled cholera, and in five minutes sent the thing to be cleansed. Cousin Robert, in his usual forethoughtful way, brought a silver service, unmarked, so that you can exchange it if you like. Do you read the papers? Do you know about Francis Hume? I found out casually from Bellamy Winthrop, who chanced to go up with him in the train. Bellamy is a ferret; that you know. He could get news out of a stone — or Francis. It seems Mr. Hume was very ill, started to come down here, was taken worse in a Concord hotel, and died there before Francis could reach him. The boy took his body and carried it to that awful camp for burial. I desire never to set eyes on the place again. I wrote to him, but he does n't answer. Good luck to you both. Regards to Captain Morton. I suppose I am to call him Ned? What with the wedding and this last nightmare, my nerves are quite unstrung.

THE DAY OF HIS YOUTH

FRANCIS HUME had gone back. It was the spring now, and a visit to the spot at that same time last year reminded me that the grass would have been thick and tall before the door, and that the linden was in bloom. I had found old Pierre in the village, and asked him to row me over; but though his arms were still like whipcords, he declined. He seemed to think the visit an intrusion upon the two who had evidently made something as holy and unapproachable in his own life as the legends of his saints. On the other hand, he was jealously unwilling to trust me there alone; and when I found another man to row me, Pierre came of his own will and took a place in the boat. The day was a heaven of May, the lake untouched. Our oars made its only ripple. It was a strange, still progress. Pierre, dark, silent, a man of thought and experience, brooded all the way, as over vanished things; and the other man evidently held him in too much awe to speak. They landed me without a word. I walked about the spot where the log-cabin had stood, now a blank in the vegetation. I lingered by the Point, to catch the little ripples there; and I visited the spring where the two men used to drink. Pierre had followed me, with the cat-like tread of the woods. He touched my sleeve, and pointed through a forest path.

"There," he said. "That is the grave."

I understood. Ernest Hume had been buried there. I walked in a few steps, and Pierre pointed. A forest of maidenhair strove and fluttered greenly. This was the grave. There was no stone to mark it; but at that moment it seemed to me very rich in peace to lie down so and to be absorbed into the life of the forest, throwing back no foolish outcry, "Here I lie! Remember."

When Pierre found that I was going back without disturbing even a leaf of

THE DAY OF HIS YOUTH

his shrine, his heart opened a little to me, and he told me a few facts of the burial. Francis Hume had brought back his father's body, and they two had dug the grave and laid him within it. Francis had never spoken. He looked like the dead. He had no mind. Pierre repeated it: he had no mind.

I could understand. He was beside himself. His soul had been reft away into merciful dulness, somewhere outside his body. When the burial was over, Francis had dismissed him and walked away into the woods. Pierre followed, silently. All that day they walked, Francis unconscious that he was not alone. Then Pierre began to realize that they were going in a great circle, and that they were coming back to the grave. Night fell, and they were still walking, now away from the grave again, but always in a circle. The moon came out, and Pierre, very hungry, yet not daring to lose sight of Francis, approached him and tried to speak; the boy's eyes were wide open, unwinking, luminous. Pierre began to talk of food, and Francis struck out at him, and walked on. Pierre followed. They continued still in the same dull circle, all night long, Francis walking like a cat undeterred by branches and avoiding pitfalls with the cleverness of the insane, and the guide, wearied and stumbling. Just as the latter darkness of night came on, Francis paused, wavered a little, and Pierre caught him as he fell. He drew him upon his shoulder, and toiled back to camp with him. There he laid him upon a couch in the cabin, and poured brandy between his lips. All that day the boy slept, only stirring when Pierre roused him to administer milk or brandy; but at twilight time he moved and opened his eyes. Pierre knew he had "come back." Then the old man placed bread and meat beside him and went silently out. He had much experience, I judged, of the dignity of the soul;

THE DAY OF HIS YOUTH

much knowledge, gained from lonely living, of her needs. He knew when she must be alone. Yet he watched all night in the grove, his quick ears strained for a movement of the creature within. What came next, Francis Hume only can tell.

IT is two o'clock in the morning, and I am writing here in the cabin doorway. I have no light, yet I can see what I am writing. That, I remember, is not what ordinarily happens; but it seems quite natural. I must write in haste, for, as I judge, I have been crazy, and now I am sane; and I must put down something to remember, lest madness should come on again. I must have something to hold to, if I am to fall back into the great confusion and trouble of mind that have been sweeping me down like a sea. For I have learned something. It is most precious, and I must be sure to keep it. There is no doubt that I have killed my father. I was not by to tend him. When his soul was going forth, I let it go alone. I brought upon him the sharpest pangs of his mortality. But even that is well. Can I write what has befallen me, to recall it to my later mind when the vision has faded, as it may? I cling to it. I must try. First, I went down into hell. I do not know much about that. It is confused. And hell is not very important. We dig it for ourselves. Let me remember only the things of God. Then I awoke, and Pierre was feeding me. He went out, and I saw the twilight shaft of light strike across the cabin where it used to fall. But I knew everything was changed. The cabin was not real. Only I was real — and Pierre. My soul — was it my soul? — went out of the cabin, and swept across Lone Mountain to the sea, and over the sea and back again. She saw the great earth swing in space. She knew there are many worlds beside. She felt an awe of the vastness of things, and she began to be healed. Then she came back to me, and I took her in, like a dove with dew upon her wings, and she comforted me. Me? Was it she who went, or I? What is she? I do not know. But I was comforted. Then, as I lay there, vision after vision began to throng upon me, and the cabin walls lifted up, and let me see the world. And I looked upon the great balances wherein we are held, and millions of souls, uncounted souls, in myriads, like little points of light, fleeing home to God. That was it —God. That was what I had sinned and suffered for, to know Him. I saw the souls going toward Him, and an ineffable delight took hold on me because I felt that I was going, too; not my body, not even the Me that stayed in the cabin, though every impulse of me was tending fast that way. I knew a flower's feeling when its fragrance meets the sun. This was love; and immediately I understood everything that it was necessary for me to understand. I comprehended His perfect well-wishing toward us. I knew one blood ran from His heart through ours. I knew how small a thing it is to say "*I* suffer." I? What is I? A mote in the whole, an aching nerve in one great plexus. And the whole will some day be nourished, and we shall be healed. I do not know whether I can believe this when I read it by day; but the cabin is thronged with — radiances. I have not learned what to call them, but they are infinitely beautiful, patient, strong, and they uphold me. I cannot think they suffer with me; their wisdom is too great. But they crowd about me silently, forbearingly, divinely. They are incarnate love. I stretch out my hands to them. While they stay, I am almost happy. I do not see them, yet they shed a lustre and the soul perceives it. I have learned — what have I learned? Obedience. I must not strive nor cry. I must serve. What? I do not know. But I must serve, even in the dark and enchained. I am content to grope, with my eyes bandaged. Content? No, this is joy. I have tasted God. I drink no other spring.

I have read this over. It is all wrong, all poor and pale; I have told nothing. Yet the visions — they are in my soul. I throw my arms about them and hold them fast. Perhaps even they must be withdrawn. Perhaps it is a part of my service to lose my way. Even that I accept. I reach my hand for the cup — thirstily. I drink, and to the Unknown God. What is He? I am contented not to know. What am I? It is His will I should not know. Only this: the soul is perfect, indestructible, and she goes to lave herself in Him.

THE next morning, said Pierre, Francis made swift preparations for going away. They were few, for he wished to retain nothing belonging to his former life. He took last long looks about the walls, he studied the pictures as if he would learn them by heart, and laid his hand upon one and another of the things that had been dear to him. Then he touched fire to the building, and stood by outside, waiting while it burned. Pierre very plainly understood why he did it, though he could not tell. He seemed to distrust the quality of my intelligence because I asked primitive questions. Was it because Francis feared marauders? Was it some idea of sacrifice to his father's memory? Was it because he felt himself unworthy to retain the precious surroundings of a life to which he had been false? As I became insistent, Pierre grew dumb. The cabin burned, he said. Francis watched it. Then he went away. He never came back.

In the old man's countenance I fancied I could trace, under a veiling patience, the lines of an immortal grief. Francis,

THE DAY OF HIS YOUTH

I could understand, had been the child of his heart, his one human love. It had taken all the great austerity of the forest to teach him to bear that loss. Yet you could see from his face, as in the faces of so many who suffer with dignity, that he was not destitute of hope.

It has been surprisingly difficult to follow the after-track of Francis Hume. For those who knew him have only to say that he disappeared. But he disappeared merely by settling down at their own door: the back-door where carriages never come. He selected a very poor and sordid street in the city where he had met his loss, and betook himself there to live; not, I believe, with any idea of work among the poor, but because he had probed life to the bottom in his own experience, and he felt constrained to seek a lower depth. He had acquired that passionate abnegation which is the child of grief; not undervaluing the joys of time, he had learned that they were not for him. Now his life became very simple, very humble, in the expectancy of its attitude; for he leaned upon God, and waited until he should be told what to do. There are strange, vivid memories of him among the people with whom he walked. Evidently he gave munificently, yet from such austerity of life, and with such directness of speech and action, that few presumed to bleed him further. In that same dark region remain to-day strange touches of magnificence and beauty; a great picture here, a glowing curtain there, dowered with a richness the present owners may not understand, although they dimly feel it. He had no formulated idea of charity, no recognition of the fact that there are theories of doing good. All that can be discovered about his later life is that he was much beloved, and that he loved much; the latter, from an aching sense of the pain common to all souls, a sense of spiritual kinship. At least, he was spared many of the taw-

THE DAY OF HIS YOUTH

dry temptations of youth; for grief had touched him so near that she had opened his eyes to the foolishness of vain desires. He could watch the fluttering of the garment of happiness without wondering if happiness were really underneath. He had seen the real; thenceforth, for him, there was no illusion. He simply lived, and shared when the inner voice told him to share; and as it afterwards proved, he made his will, and left his fortune to buy great tracts of pine woods for a camping-ground forevermore. But that does not pertain to his story. Sufficient to know that the trust has been very wisely administered, and that hundreds of squalid creatures were last summer turned loose there.

Meantime Zoe Morton was fulfilling to the letter her own cynical prophecy of an unhappy marriage. There is no doubt whatever about the life she led with Captain Morton. He was a frank materialist. Every man has his price, said he;

every woman also. The baser breed of vices are as unavoidable as any other part of the earthly scheme. Eat and drink — and die when you must. He was kind enough to Zoe in the manner of a man who would not wantonly hurt his horse or dog; he would have been kinder had she not rebelled. But after the manner of her sex and nature, when they wed with Bottom, she went hysterical-mad. He got tired — and he rode away. Then, after five years of marriage and two of acute invalidism, thus she wrote Francis Hume: —

I SEND this to the Boston post-office in the hope of finding you. My aunt thinks she saw you in the street the other day; but I did not need that to tell me you were here. I have guessed it for a long time. I have almost felt you knew how I suffer. I am asking an impossible service. Captain Morton is abroad, and he refuses to come home. I am dying, and he will not believe it. I have written him and cabled him; but I have said I was dying for the last three years. Now it is true. Will you go over there and see him? *Make him believe it.* Make him come to me. I do not know how — but make him. His bankers are Baring Bros. Perhaps they can tell you where he is.

DEAR LADY, — I start to-night. It was generous of you to ask me. He shall come. *Francis Hume to Zoe Montrose*

BUT Captain Morton was not to be found, either in England or on the Continent; and so there was much delay which must have tried the soul of the messenger beyond endurance. Through one of the foolish ironies of life, the captain ("rather fat," six years before!)

had decided, in a futile blindness to his own limitations, to join an exploring party to the interior of Abyssinia. He had always a childish vanity; perhaps that led him to ignore all the habits of his luxurious past and seek healthier living through the means he had despised. Thus to nourish himself for more vices! So does the *bon vivant* recuperate at Spas.

Thither, as soon as Francis Hume could get upon his track, he followed him, through danger and delay, through wilderness and night. The difficulties of the journey were a thousandfold enhanced by his ignorance of any definite route; and he made many a maddening detour and experienced tragic loss in the treachery of guides. This, at least, is apparent from some crumpled notes of travel found among his possessions. At length, suddenly, dramatically, he came upon his man. What arguments he used, no one can say. Perhaps Morton had grown sick of his fool's errand, perhaps his heart was really touched, at last ; but he did turn about and make all due speed to America. Francis accompanied him only to the fastest steamer route; and then dropped off to take another boat home. His notes keep rigid silence concerning the captain. Did he hate him to the last, or had hatred, like other spawn of evil, sunk, for him, in the unplumbed depths of larger seas? Captain Morton came home and found his wife still living. She died within a week, and there is a strange contradiction in her end. The nurse who was with her says that she moaned for him, like a child, through all those dreary days; and yet when he came into the room she looked at him, turned her face to the wall, and would not speak. It seemed almost as if she had held herself within a bond she loathed, and as if death had really freed her.

Francis returned to Boston on his slow-sailing boat. They were coming up the harbor in the flush of twilight, and the State-house dome stood like a golden beehive against the sky. He had kept very much to himself, said one of the passengers who was strongly drawn to him, and now he stood by the rail, not looking forward with the seeking glance of those whose voyage is done, but musingly into the sea. A little sailboat had been keeping alongside. Two men were in it, and they were plainly drunk. They had a little rough dog, and they were teasing him. The passengers looked on with indignant protest. One or two called out; but the men swore back and bullied him the more. Their last pleasantry was to hold him over the side with a feint of dropping him; and suddenly, in an access of cruelty, they called out that he should swim for it. And then they dropped him. Francis Hume had not followed the entire occurrence; but the passenger who told it happened to glance at him at the moment when the

THE DAY OF HIS YOUTH

dog was thrown overboard. That he saw. She says he glowed at once with pure anger. His face lighted and flamed; and two seconds after the dog went down, Francis Hume sprang after him. There was an outcry on the instant. A boat was lowered, but some strange clumsiness of execution seemed to overshadow the whole thing; so that Hume had to keep himself afloat for what seemed a long time. In reality, she supposes, it was minutes. That was nothing. Miles of swimming were nothing to a man of his training; but when the boat reached him, he threw the dog into it and himself slipped away. That was all. The event is confused in the minds of everybody present, and no one can wholly account for it. It seemed fatality. He simply went down, and his body was not recovered. The men in the sailboat, shocked into soberness, put about, and left the steamer in all possible haste; and the passenger who told me the story dried the little dog in her shawl and promised him a home. But of this thing every one is convinced. Francis Hume must have gone willingly to his death, but he did not choose it. The sailors of the rescuing boat say that his face showed a strange bewilderment, but no refusal of their efforts; he did not mean to drown. There must have been, said the ship's doctor, some lesion of the heart.

Much as I know of the reality of his life (and it ended not so long ago), it never seems to me to belong to this actual world, this "city by the sea." For me, its mirror lies, strangely enough, in another life of noble ends and uncompleted action: Beauchamp's Career. There is your only parallel, even to the splendid futility of its close. Read this from Meredith's novel, which is, after all, nothing less than vivid biography, and fit it to the end of Francis Hume.

"An old man volunteered the information. 'That's the boy. That boy was

THE DAY OF HIS YOUTH

in his father's boat out there, with two of his brothers, larking; and he and another, older than him, fell overboard; and just then Commander Beauchamp was rowing by, and I saw him from off here, where I stood, jump up and dive, and he swam to his boat with one of them, and got him in safe: that boy; and he dived again after the other, and was down a long time. Either he burst a vessel or he got cramp, for he'd been rowing himself from the schooner grounded down at the river-mouth, and must have been hot when he jumped in; either way, he fetched the second up, and sank with him. Down he went.'

"A fisherman said: . . . 'Do you hear that voice thundering? That's the great Lord Romfrey. He's been directing the dragging since five o' the evening, and will till he drops or drowns, or up comes the body.'

"'O God, let's find the body!' the woman with the little boy called out.

THE DAY OF HIS YOUTH

"'... My lord! my lord!' sobbed the woman, and dropped on her knees.

"'What's this?' the earl said, drawing his hand away from the woman's clutch at it.

"'She's the mother, my lord,' several explained to him.

"'Mother of what?'

"'My boy,' the woman cried, and dragged the urchin to Lord Romfrey's feet, cleaning her boy's face with her apron.

"'It's the boy Commander Beauchamp drowned to save,' said a man.

"All the lights of the ring were turned on the head of the boy. ... The boy struck out both arms to get his fists against his eyelids.

"This is what we have in exchange for Beauchamp.

"It was not uttered, but it was visible in the blank stare at one another of the two men who loved Beauchamp, after they had examined the insignificant bit of mud-bank life remaining in this world in the place of him."

BUT those of us who loved Francis Hume do not ask to find his body, even for tender burial. We only pray that in some bright star-passage we may be fortunate, and one day see his soul.

www.ingramcontent.com/pod-product-compliance
Lightning Source LLC
Chambersburg PA
CBHW030358170426
43202CB00010B/1419